Living for Learning

Living for Learning

Terence Chivers

Copyright © 2015 by Terence Chivers.

Library of Congress Control Number: 2015902651
ISBN: Hardcover   978-1-4990-9556-2
              Softcover   978-1-4990-9433-6
              eBook   978-1-4990-9557-9

All rights reserved. No part of this book may be reproduced or transmitted in any form or by any means, electronic or mechanical, including photocopying, recording, or by any information storage and retrieval system, without permission in writing from the copyright owner.

Any people depicted in stock imagery provided by Thinkstock are models, and such images are being used for illustrative purposes only.
Certain stock imagery © Thinkstock.

Print information available on the last page.

Rev. date: 03/03/2015

To order additional copies of this book, contact:
Xlibris
800-056-3182
www.Xlibrispublishing.co.uk
Orders@Xlibrispublishing.co.uk

Contents

Autobiography Synopsis ix

Chapter 1   Introduction – Why Write a Life Story? 1

Chapter 2   Origins 4

Chapter 3   Happy Childhood 10

Chapter 4   Various kinds of learning 16

Chapter 5   Life in the War 22

Chapter 6   Psychic experiences 28

Chapter 7   Leaving Home 31

Chapter 8   Nurse or Goaler? 40

Chapter 9   From Heat to Light 52

Chapter 10 The Education Saga 65

Chapter 11 Family 74

Chapter 12 A key influence 78

Chapter 13 Motivating Influences 83

Chapter 14 Last thoughts 89

Dedication:

To the Morya Federation for
the enlightenment it inspires

Terence Stafford Chivers, (born 4.6.1930)

Autobiography Synopsis

Place of birth: 16 Cavenham Gdns., Romford, Essex, England.
Father: Charles Henry Chivers
Mother: Winifred Beatrice Chivers (nee Hart)
Elder brother: Vernon Terence Chivers (born 22.8.1928)

T.S. Chivers

1935: Salisbury Road Infants and Junior Schools in Gidea Park, Romford till age 10 years (1941) Then one year in a private school in Romford to retake the 11+ examination.

1942-1946: free place in local grammar school – Royal Liberty School.

1946: first post – Marshalls Food Products in the City of London. Left home to live in London, (Pimlico).

1948: Conscription. Registered conscientious objector. Two years hospital service at Charing Cross Hospital, London.

1950: entered psychiatric nurse training at Bethlam Royal Hospital, Kent. Lived in. Quit after a few months.

1951: Several months in the Ritz Hotel In London's west end. Then moved into Charing Cross Hospital as a trainee cook. Became qualified (City and Guilds 151 certificate in trade cooking – a one-year crash course by evening study. Living with friends again in Pimlico.

1954 : moved to St. Thomas's hospital group as a chef in charge of a small women's hospital in London.

1956: entered Peace News, the pacifist newspaper. Living now on my own in various flats in London.

1958: married Barbara Josephine Killingback, a school teacher. Moved to a flat in Ealing Broadway, London.

1959: started part-time sociology course at Regent Street Polytechnci, London,

1960: entered Greater London Council as a clerk in the education department at County Hall, Westminster, London. This gave me time in the evenings for the degree level study and improved my wages. My wife and I obtained a mortgage and were now living in a maisonette in Ponders Ends, Middlesex.

1962: my wife got a teaching job in Stevenage (Herdforshire) which enabled us to claim a new terraced house in this new town. I was much involved in the local Campaign for Nuclear Disarmament group over several years.

1964: graduated BSc(Soc) degree, 2:2 hons. University of London. Became lecturer in General Studies at Lechworth College of Technology in Hertfordshire.

1966: birth of a daughter – Alison
Success with a qualifying examination to permit study for a part-time masters degree (London University).

1968: MSc(Econ) – a second sociology degree specialising in occupations, London University at Regent street Polytechnic. Upgraded at the college to senior lecturer in sociology when I move to Birmingham Polytechnic. We live now in Mosley, Birmingham.

1971: Daughter starts at the local infants school. She seems very unhappy so we move her to a nearby fee-paying school. Calmness descends on the household again.

1972: PhD in sociology based on a study of chefs and cooks in the commercial and hospital kitchens. External degree, London University.

1973: move to Sunderland Polytechnic as principal lecturer in sociology. We live first in Cleadon and then move into Sunderland. My work consists of developing and then teaching sociology in degree and diploma courses.

1975: Wife no longer able to offer sexual contact. I evaluated the situation and decided to accept it. Daughter doing well at fee-paying school.

1984-1988: daughter graduates from Kings College, London University with 2:1 in German.

1991: retired August 31. Daughter married and living in London. Wife and I retire to a detached bungalow in Goring-by-Sea on the South Coast.

Re-enter Arcane School. Pass through stages of studentship and become a secretary helping to teach students in the School.

1992: Some fee paying sociology teaching. Formed core group to set up Worthing University of the Third Age (U3A). We offer low cost, unpaid teaching on a range of subjects.

1993: one-year Certificate in Life History Work. University of Sussex. I teach sociology and begin the life story writing group for Worthing U3A. I become Secretary of Worthing U3A

1994: registered for DPhil (Autobiography and Life Review) with the Institute of Professional and Continuing Education, Sussex University.

1995: Daughter moves to Sydney, Australia with husband and daughter. We commence Christmas visits and holidays to Australia.

1996: I am elected to represent West Sussex U3As on the West Sussex Adult Education Forum which advises the county's adult education officer.

1997: a member takes over as secretary of Worthing U3A. It had proved difficult to find a member to take on the job.

1998: Award of DPhil. It had been submitted in September the previous year.

2005: Disagreement with the London Arcane School staff over whether to approach members in order to seek a group to launch issues of wider study in the Alice Bailey writings. A colleague and I begin methodical review of a *Treatise on Cosmic Fire*, (Lucis Press, 1989). Same review repeated a second time. A small group forms.

2009: founding of Morya Federation under the principal guidance of Michael Robbins though many of the members are leaders of groups of aspirants and would-be disciples of the ageless wisdom. Full range of Alice Bailey's writings studied. I become one of the mentors.

2014: My wife dies in the final phase of Alzheimer's disease.

Chapter One

Introduction — Why Write a Life Story?

Introduction to Life Story Writing

I have called autobiography life story writing at this stage because I have been told by those who write their own story that it sounds less imposing and perhaps rather less demanding from the point of view of a writer. But less demanding in what sense? I would accept this only in the sense that it is perhaps less something produced by an established writer. You may/may not be such. But for the purposes I would urge you to consider, the quality of your composition matters little. What then is the goal of a life story? I believe that there is one overall and demanding goal. That is - learning, i.e. what you can learn in the process.

One might then ask: what is the use of learning if you write your life story late in life? Assuming you write you story in your final years it may be too late to begin trying to live out any corrections. Nonetheless, some people may still wish to try. Moreover, life story writing is not confined to old age; it can be done at any age. In addition, many people, not just those living in or deriving from the Orient, accept the concept of reincarnation. The purpose of writing one's life story, and rewriting it throughout one's life is then apparent, for living is a learning process, even if it is possible to learn very little, possibly even nothing at some stages. The continuing learner during life and between lives is the soul, which is a life that each of us possesses. By all means refer to the internet if you would know more about these fascinating subjects - reincarnation, soul.

My task here is to try to give some kind of impression concerning the nature of the learning that can develop. This kind of learning has to do with the nature of the person, i.e. how they respond during interaction with other people, how they view situations involving the other kingdoms: mineral, vegetable and animal, their orientation towards political, economic and social differences. We all have to learn how to orient ourselves to such situations and how to respond to them when involved. I assume that it is best to be able to respond to situations creatively, i.e. helpfully, in ways which enable other people to become helpful and willing to aid society. In other words, the intention is to orient oneself towards a policy of goodwill and seek to foster a similar attitude in those with whom we interact. By so doing we develop a soul orientation, which, if persistently followed, will lead to soul consciousness. This we seek because that is the goal of human evolution, which when attained, will lead on to increasingly spiritual development. Then the great evils of the world will gradually disappear. No more war, poverty, torture, social discrimination, etc. We have the power to change the world and the place to start is with ourselves.

People who are so minded can opt for caring jobs, such as nursing, medicine, social work, teaching, etc. Such caring activity can be helpful to society. However, the vast majority of jobs will provide opportunities for the outlook of goodwill.

How does life story writing develop this goal? A clear learning stance can be a step in the right direction. What is this type of learning? It is willingness to assess one's life dispassionately, neither condemning nor condoning activities and responses by yourself and others. Rather one notes events, situations, attitudes and actions.

One is aware of them as of acceptable or unacceptable quality but one minimises the feelings attached to them because the power of emotions makes situations difficult to evaluate in terms of soul values, and these are the values we must use for assessment. We need to learn to listen to situations, watch happenings, evaluate motives and appreciate kind intentions. We must seek to understand complexities and recognise careful and careless thought in others as well as ourselves. Learning then is a process requiring skill and thoroughness. And honesty! Often we will be faced with mixed motives. It is important to recognise this rather than being satisfied with the dominant one. Moreover, action is not necessarily based on one dominant motive. Often, what is done is based on several motives, sometimes consciously, sometimes unconsciously.

It should be clear then, that learning is likely to be a complex task and will make definite calls on our ability.

But why write it down? Why develop it as a life story? Because learning also involves recognition, recognition of our personalities and of our ability to act in accordance with the soul. Writing all this down formalises learning and that is a necessary outcome. Writing it down enables us to return to our views and re-evaluate them and we may wish to do this from time to time. Bear in mind that writing is not the sole method of life story writing. You might want to paint it, write a song about it or a poem or a saga. The best method is the one which most suits you.

I hope I have persuaded some of my readers to make a start. If you feel I can help you, you will find me willing t do so as best I can: terence.chivers1@ntlworld.com. To give some degree of help I have set out my own life story in what follows. The final chapter returns to the issue of learning again.

Chapter Two

Origins

Bear with me while I set the scene, not my own, nor that of my parents but rather than of their parents. That will clarify my origins. My father's father was Charles Henry Chivers, whom I knew as a shortish, rotund man, who owned a hardware shop in the East End of London. He married a woman whose background was in domestic employment. Their first venture in procreation brought about my father, who, as if to confirm his origins, also became Charles Henry Chivers. Next to arrive on the scene was a daughter – Edith. I say a daughter with a trace of doubt because by the time I knew her, she, was the size of two, and was wont to talk about landing those, who incurred her displeasure, with "a fourpenny one". A vast forearm was waved before our eyes and one felt some sympathy for those at the receiving end. Once she fell in the sea at Southend when the family said that she caused something of tidal wave.

I cannot be entirely sure that granddad owned his shop but it seems likely because he had made some money selling glue to furniture makers in the area. I remember him as an elderly, quiet man with a moustache, who had to watch his pace due to a heart condition. Sadly, one day in his sixties he didn't. He ran to catch a bus. He got on it upright but was carried off lengthwise. The funeral followed. Grandmother, his wife, was loud and tactless, with speech that was distinctly working class. She was decidedly stingy when it came to spending. Her other distinguishing feature was her superstitiousness. This was so pronounced that one had to take care not to laugh.

The parents on my mother's side were a different story. The father was a failed businessman who had to accept a job as a church verger in order to raise his two daughters. He was middle class and married to a woman of the same class. Before his demise, there had been servants in the house. My grandfather's business failure must have come as a considerable shock because the entire family sank into an impoverished lifestyle. This may help to explain my mother's and grandmother's trait of snobbery. They looked down on the Chivers, yet in social terms, the Chivers, or their like, was the best they could expect for their daughters. In fact, both daughters married men of working class origin. I think it would be true to say that both grandmother and mother looked down on persons of lower social standing because these two relations of mine needed a sense of social superiority.

As a young man, my father was somewhat short-tempered. He was a City of London import-export clerk who commuted every weekday to his office which, save for a few months with another firm after his wartime Navy experience, he never left. He was a one-employer man, from leaving school till retirement, aged 80. In the end it was the dawn of the computer which dislodged him, when the firm eased him out in order to bring in a man with excellent references but no nous. The new man's computer references suggested that he could computerise the accounts. That had impressed the firm. But it was not a good move for them. After some months, the firm had to bribe the chap to leave. But by that time, the computer was in and father was out. However, father was accorded an occupational pension, which his widow could continue to draw at half rate.

Father was a stalwart Toc H man, and a great church-goer, while mother was half-hearted in this respect. The Church played an important part in his life. From his descriptions of his background one gathered that his church friends had helped him as a young man to steer his activities into a respectable lifestyle. Therefore, the Church assumed for him a place of moral guidance.

When war broke out in 1939, it was not long before father had joined the Air-Raid Precautions force. That was apt to keep him busy at nights putting out incendiary bombs. We lived in Romford, Essex and, being so near to London we had to put up with incessant bombing. This we expected but father's conscription at the age of forty came as a surprise. He joined the Navy serving on naval protection vessels in the Thames. The job was to prevent, or at least warn of enemy infiltration up the river. He enjoyed the outdoor life and camaraderie of naval activity. But for mother, I think, instead of being demobilised, he would have stayed put when the war ended.

Right into his old age, my father retained his active mind, always interested in the world around him and with a child-like wonder concerning it. For example, he would look at a churchyard and marvel at the number of people buried there. Had he been born in post-World War II Britain, instead of 1901, he would have gone to university, and studied geography or perhaps history. As it was he read mostly westerns and concerned himself with improving his paltry investments. However, he had enough perception to know what he had missed in educational terms and often talked of the opportunities available to young people with a sense of critical envy.

Mother seems to have married in order to have children. Her own were her abiding passion. She devoted herself to her two boys with a profound love. Her constant thought was how she could ensure that no danger ever came their way – a somewhat difficult objective during wartime. On marriage, she gave up her work as a shop assistant in London's West End to give all her time to the home. She kept a clean place without being house-proud. The love she conferred on her two boys would have been difficult to better.

She was something of a contrast to father in that she used her mind so little. Yet the mind was there and she could use it when she wanted. The truth of the matter was that she had decided not to bother with thought more than was required for daily living. She found mothering emotions far more attractive. Here I think she was unsurpassed in her devotion to her sons.

One might sum up the home as a good one. My brother and I were well cared for and got whatever mother could afford. It was a typical lower middle class home, a terraced house bought with a mortgage on a new housing development in Romford. My brother and I got on reasonably well though there was a fair amount of quarrelling. He had a more outgoing temperament than me. As a child and young man, I was painfully introverted. Another quality which remained with me for a long time was my incomprehension at the behaviour of others. I can recall sitting in my pram watching my brother howling over some frustration and thinking how strange it was that he should behave in that way.

Our mother being so caring led to her two boys being spoilt. There was discipline at times, occasionally forcible. But mostly mother would talk to us and persuade us into more reasonable activities. As we grew into young children, the institution of the family outing took us on a variety of country outings. I remember Noak Hill, Havering and Harrow Weald of places visited. These walks were apt to be prolonged by father's desire to find a short cut, almost invariably leading to our getting lost. As we achieved our teens, the walks were replaced by cycle rides and this helped my brother and I to escape our mother's ever watchful and protective eye.

The family grew up with a succession of pets. We had several cats at different times. They all seemed to succumb to canker for which there seemed to be little treatment in those days. We had a succession of dogs too. One female one escaped one day from the house and got what she wanted from a male dog. Presumably, it was all rather painful because as he withdrew his penis, she let out some piercing screams alerting a neighbouring lady in a house opposite:

> "What's all that noise?" she asked.
> "Oh it's only our dog, I said.
> "But why is it making all that noise?" The lady was not lacking in persistence.
> "She's been with another dog" I said, wishing I could vanish.
> "But why does that lead her to make that noise?" the lady continued.

So it went on for another few minutes. The trouble was that, though I knew perfectly well what had happened, I lacked the vocabulary adequate to explain it with propriety. I was only ten. In the end, the lady seemed to grasp the situation, probably due to my embarrassment. So she withdrew and I fled back indoors. I wonder how often adults fail to realise children's lack of vocabulary.

It was a happy home. The two boys and their mother had a close and warm relationship. I think that father felt that mother had transferred too much affection to her boys. However, he mellowed as he got older and, by our teens, he was friendly towards his sons. We could talk to him as we did to mother. I can remember, in my teens, remarking on this change. His explanation was: "You learn a lot as you get older."

Mother remained totally dedicated to mothering. She told my brother and I that she had no time for sexuality. In her view, the whole business was entirely uninteresting. I think mother's attitude lay in her commitment to self-control. Only her mothering emotions were given free reign. Her physical actions were entirely under her command. Father seemed to accept her sex disinterest; at least he never mentioned it. Moreover, he showed complete loyalty to mother when the two boys left home.

What the home lacked was any depth of education. Though both parents could read and write, neither had experienced more than the primary education of their day. However, what they lacked in knowledge was made up for in mother's determination for upward social mobility for her sons. Money was found to send my brother to a school to learn clerical skills such as bookkeeping and shorthand and when she found that I had not been selected for grammar schooling, I was dispatched to a private school so that I could have a second try at the examination for selective schooling. To mother's delight I was successful this second time.

I need now to consider my childhood in rather more detail – the subject of the next chapter.

Chapter Three

Happy Childhood

I was born in 1930 and brought up in Gidea Park which is part of Romford in Essex. In my childhood days there was a market there at least once a week to which farm animals were brought for sale. Every now and again a bull would escape, doubtless trying to avert its Oxo-cube fate. The errant animal usually caused quite a stir among shoppers and drivers. But it was a short-lived flurry of activity before the animal was captured. We would also see farm animals when the family went out for walks in the countryside at weekends.

These were family outings – father and mother and their two sons, plus whatever dog we had at the time. I do not think the two boys found the walks exciting but we believed in their health-giving properties. Most of our time outside the house was spent in the garden – quite a reasonable size, about twenty yards long and six wide.

My brother was the best part of two years older than me so he was bigger and stronger. Outside the home, he was more likely than me to start the activities between us. In the garden, his favourite pastime was digging holes. It was the different coloured sands which seemed to fascinate him. With my assistance we could get down several feet without too much difficulty. Games would often revolve round these holes. There would be charging and parrying with sticks.

One day my brother said that if I charged him while he defended the hole he would not budge. We had recently seen a film where the attack took the form of a man flying feet first at his opponent. I said that my brother would never dare stand his ground if I did this. He said that I would never dare throw myself feet first at him. I was determined to show him that I could keep my word. So I took a long run and proceeded towards him, feet first, body horizontal. Of course, he simply sidestepped and I ended up in the hole, with every drop of air knocked out of me. A well known motto is 'He who dares wins'. Maybe so when there is proper forethought!

Another favourite garden activity was riding our bikes. It could not have done the garden much good but mother would not allow us to play in the street, so the garden was all that was available for outdoor activity. There were a couple of Comice pear trees which regularly yielded fruit. Yet the fruit never seemed to ripen so we used to use them to throw at each other. There were, too, soft fruit bushes. But they were never pruned or fed and just grew wild. Father added some plumb trees in due course. Yet he took little notice of them. Perhaps that is why they produced so little fruit.

A further pastime, led by mother, was the pictures – as the cinema was referred to. Her particular penchant was for horror films. When she could not find anyone else to accompany her, she was wont to trot off to a dilapidated cinema nearby. Its projector was old and decrepit. So just as the film reached the really scary bits, the projector was wont to breakdown. The result was that parts of the film were omitted by the time the projector was persuaded to fulfil its function. Hence if we asked about the film the next day, mother's account left something to be desired. We might query:

> "What happened then mum? The monster was free again and fighting the werewolf: who won?"

She might reply: "Well, I don't really know how it worked out because the projector broke down at that stage."
We persisted: "But it must have restarted."
But mother was truthful: "Yes, but that bit was missed out when it started again."
"Oh mum!"

In contrast to my brother's domination of play outside the home so I was the leader of play inside the home. Much of this focused on toy animals to which we assigned characters, largely derived from our reading. I used to make up endless stories to do with these characters played out with the animals as persons. This activity would take up many an hour.

My father's interest was more towards the theatre than the cinema. He particularly favoured the musical shows with song and dance routines. He seemed to like it all, and the family would be taken from time-to-time to London for one of these colourful events. Not that I enjoyed them. At home, he had acquired a liking for billiards. He even bought a half-sized billiard table which was installed in the front room. He used to play one of his two boys, whenever he found us available. Yet despite his interest in the game, he nearly always lost, but that did not deter him.

There were periodic visits to our various relations. Grandma (mother's mother) had a house in Allfarthing Lane, Wandsworth in London and though we liked her, we found the house creepy. To this house on occasion would come grandma's sisters and a brother. All the sisters were spinsters At least two of these sisters had considerable drawing skills and left behind a number of sketches when they died. This certainly proved that skills are not passed on since there was no such ability in our family. I should have needed individual teacher attention to be able to draw even the simplest of outlines. Yet no teachers in any school I passed through ever seemed to consider such basic work necessary.

My father's parents we would sometimes visit at Christmas. They lived over their hardware shop in London. The shop was located in the East End, which, at that time, seemed often to be full of drunks, which made us glad to reach our grandparents' premises without incident. I can remember a little about the meals. It was mostly turkey with lashings of thick gravy. This would be followed by Christmas pudding, the consumption of which was accompanied by tension. The trouble was that Grandma Chivers would put threepenny bits in the pudding and mother was terrified that her sons might swallow them.

Like most children of the time, we picked up whatever diseases were around. My brother was really very ill with scarlet fever and was taken into hospital, where he picked up a secondary infection. Mother saw this as a test of her motherly dedication. Arriving at the hospital she scooped him out of bed and brought him home in a taxi. With her nursing, he gradually improved. I managed to catch most of the diseases around. But a weak digestion seems to have been a problem all my own.

At mealtimes over the weekend, we all came together. The Sunday joint was very much an institution and one that little appealed to me since it was usually mutton, which was not to my taste. I imagine that the choice of mutton was cheapness but it tended to be tough when roasted. Snack food like cheese was more to my taste. My brother would tuck into puddings but I was little interested. Generally, I was a picky eater, apt to leave a good deal of a meal on my plate.

Food storage in those days was primitive compared to today. Freezers had not been invented and only wealthy people could afford refrigerators. Hence food for most families was stored in a larder. This was a kind of cupboard. The wooden shelves would be lined with paper and the food placed on them. The typical larder was ventilated with a grid containing small holes. Flies could sometimes gain access so food items had to be covered in some way.

Because the ability to keep food fresh was limited, shopping had to be carried out every day. Mother mostly shopped at the local

Co-operative Wholesale Society shop which was close by. Milk could be bought there but, like many families, milk was delivered to us daily. The milkman would call for payment on a Friday. Mostly, we had the money ready. But on one to two occasions my brother or I would answer the door to 'explain' that mother was 'out' and the bill would have to wait a week. This little 'drama' took place in our two-up two-down terraced house with a scullery and upstairs bathroom. There was also a little box room. Downstairs, one room served as living room-cum-dining room. Alongside this was the front room which was reserved for 'best'. That meant that this room was set aside for anyone who might call. However, visitors were few so this room with its carpet square and high backed chairs stood largely unused in what we thought of as solitary splendour.

The other rooms had linoleum on the floors. It was quite presentable but mighty cold to unslippered feet that had hopped out of bed in the morning. None of the family aspired to slippers, nor dressing gowns, to name another common item of home apparel, i.e. common enough today. One went to the bathroom in the mornings in one's underwear and decidedly chilly it was since central heating was for the wealthy only. The only fire of the house would be in the living room. As it was a coal fire, it had to be started each morning with paper and wood. The scullery was the only other warm room.

As ours was a terraced house, there were neighbours on either side. We 'knew' few – i.e. exchanged greetings with one or two neighbours in both directions. Just occasionally one got to know someone from a little further down the road or 'opposite' as the other side of the road was called. This happened in respect of a family opposite, fairly well visible from our front room. Towards the end of the war the lady of this house was inspired to start street parties.

However, this neighbourly activity was coupled with a generous attitude towards the milkman. It all began with tips for him but developed into the offer of tea. This gave way to his access to the house -- for which he seemed to have his own key. Our mother looked askance!

Such then was our suburban lifestyle. We accepted and practised the distant friendliness towards neighbours - a polite kind of coolness, not too close since that could lead to disputes. For the most part, people kept themselves to themselves and, apart from the lady across the road, there was little heterosexual activity, except between married couples of course. There were enough children to believe in that. Homosexual activity was unheard of.

How might I characterise my childhood? I think the proper word is 'dreamy'. I dreamed my way through primary school. I was apt to be in a kind of perpetual reverie, dreaming about mother and the home. Moreover, I was a very shy little boy, sensitive and timid. I guess I was what some people would call a 'mother's darling'. That would not have worried me; I was never bothered about other people's views concerning me. However it is true that I found primary school a shock. The big surprise was the way the other children behaved. There seemed to be so much fighting, sneering and shouting.

In respect of the home, I would call it happy. I was satisfied with its suburban lifestyle since I knew nothing else.

Time now, to tell you a little more about my schooling.

Chapter Four

Various kinds of learning

I quickly realised that I did not like school. My mother left me at the school gate and I had to mix with other children. They, like me, were infants, mostly about five years old, They were not particularly friendly. The girls took delight in pinching other children and this would interrupt my reverie when they pinched me. I can remember liking one of the teachers, largely I think because she read *Winnie the Pooh (A.A. Milne)* to us. But that is about as far as my primary school memories extend.

The junior boys' school (7 to 11 years of age), which followed the infants' stage, comes more easily to mind. Perhaps the reason that I can better remember it was because I was rather more aware of the world around me by this time. The school drew on a mixed social class catchment area. I should think that rather more than half the children were from the working class, more than had been so in the infants school, probably due to the increase in a new housing estate. The boys from this social class were keen to show off their physical toughness. This was accompanied by a search for dominant physical power. What they seemed to want was the status that such power could command. All this was quite meaningless to me. So began a source of bewilderment which stayed with me till I picked up sociology during my twenties. But during school-time, their working class ostentatious seeking of macho prowess made no sense at all to me.

However, despite my puzzlement, I soon realised how to cope with the situation. One option would have been to try to join the lads. Another would have been to resist. I did neither but opted to distance myself from them while resisting their activities covertly.

So far as junior school itself was concerned I have no recollection of either liking it or being successful in it. Part of the problem was that I was still too attached to mother and therefore spent too much time daydreaming. I managed to achieve a friend towards the end of the secondary school. His conversation seemed obsessed with sex. One day, he informed me, that babies come out of the back passage. Hence one would be right to assume that his knowledge about sex was somewhat less than his interest in the subject!

Like other children I had missed quite a lot of schooling through various illnesses. I was therefore none too surprised when, like my brother before me, I did not succeed at what was called the 11+ -- which is the age when children are/are not offered a free place at local selective schools. However, my performance could not have been a complete write-off since mother felt that I merited education at a private school for a year in order to retake the scholarship examination the following year.

This private school turned out to be an eye-opener. The pupils were middle class hooligans. Looking back, I should recommend Borstal for three or four of them. They kicked and spat at the teachers and led them a terrible time. How anyone learned anything was a wonder. However, at the end of the year I re-sat the scholarship exam and was successful.

So I transferred to the all-boys grammar school: the Royal Liberty School in Hornchurch, Essex. For me, this was a transition to a different world. The entire school culture was so different to anything I had experienced within the formal education system up to that time. It was as though the entire male orientation of power had been firmly pushed into second place. Instead, the orientation was academic success. This change in culture meant that I had found a school with which I could identify.

True, there was still 'games'; the school being sport oriented – which I certainly was not. My stature was tall, thin and slight. So if I was barged at football, I would simply topple backwards. This earned no football respect if I happened to be goalie, holding the ball! I was little better at cricket. One day, while fielding at a match I was hit by a cricket ball on the head. It was a mighty six scored by a batsman in a different game some distance away. I was soon off to hospital for examination which confirmed that my head was harder than the cricket ball. So I was soon back at school, trying to work out how I could escape athletics.

Escape was possible for some of the time. I grew good at finding empty classrooms where I could secrete myself till the games period was over. However, when teaching staff were in attendance, I had to put in an appearance, and it was putting the shot, then throwing the discus or javelin. The latter carried certain dangers. Over the years, the bamboo had warped, which meant that it was far from straight. Hence this spear-like object was apt to wallop one round the back of the head as one threw it. This was dangerous not only to my head but to anyone who might be vaguely in front of me. Fortunately, my deflected javelin never seemed to find unexpected destinations.

Sadly too, there was boxing – at which I was a disaster. I had no desire to hit anyone but I was also very keen to see that no one hit me. So in the gymnasium, I would endeavour to keep my opponent as distant as possible. In action, I must have looked like a flailing machine at full power. That way I kept my opponent at a suitable distance.

Games and sport, whatever their supposed educational value simply had no contact with my view of life. I had no time for them;

my participation depended solely on their compulsory nature. Of course this earned me the reputation of being weedy among the lads. Before long I had been cast as president of the Weeds and Wild Flowers Association, a position accorded me by popular acclamation. I am pleased to say that I maintained this office uncontested, till leaving the school in 1947.

Fortunately, there were academic lessons too and a number of subjects caught my interest. I can recall writing the most diabolical rubbish for essays. I used to conjure up monsters and awful beings. I suspect the source for much of this would be comics – Beano, Dandy and the like. I absorbed a good deal of Edgar Rice-Boroughs too. Yet there was also Agatha Christie, Edgar Allen Poe and P. G. Wodehouse. Strangely, I liked English grammar, while Mathematics was my favourite. In fact, I constituted a secondary form of learning for maths: a little band of cribbers would sit near me and follow my answers. Other subjects appealed less. I found I related little to the science subjects and languages. Latin was my *bête noire*. Even so, I managed to pass the School Certificate Examination together with exemption from matriculation.

The teachers were an interesting bunch. There was the geography master who manifested wisdom but who did not want to be bothered with teaching about countries and maps. The trouble was that I was not interested in them either. The factualness of the subject seemed boring. He managed to interest himself with some astronomy and I certainly learned about night and day and the seasons. But he left learning about regions, climates, topography and the like to us boys and his recommended books. Lads like me, who needed the reinforcement of classroom discussion, were just unlucky.

There was too, 'religious studies'. This was taken by different teachers every year. The first was a little round man who talked about Spiritualism. The following year we had a woman teacher who was committed to a traditional perspective based on the Church of England. This stirred a strong sense of rejection in me. I could see no sense in the story of Jesus Christ, the Son of God and how He had been sent to overcome our sins. The notion of a personal God too, seemed ludicrous. Anyhow, her simple faith roused me, a very shy boy of 13, to speak out to explain why I rejected her views. Today I would regard this as teenage arrogance. I had every right to think that she was wrong. But I should have shown far more courtesy in how I responded to her teaching. Her response was to name several of the class who were experiencing religious commitment. That worried me not at all.

Then there was the history master, who radiated enthusiasm. Dates flew in all directions and some of us would try to slow him down. One day we were studying some historical figure and the master ruefully commented that the text book did not explain what happened to him. "Oh, it does Sir", I chirped. "It says on the next page, he died." Fortunately for me, the master was a kindly man so my stupidity was allowed to pass without comment, though there was a glance!

The French master was in some ways the worst of the bunch. Somewhere, perhaps during his own studies a certain fierceness had replaced his more human qualities. In the class there was one lad who had made it to grammar school by some kind of fluke. He simply never spoke and appeared to sit at his desk gazing into space. This situation was intolerable to the French master. He would throw down his textbook, cross the room to the lad and beat him up. Then he would explain to the class that he wanted the lad to take up the issue of the beating so that the matter of the lad's being in the school could be brought to a head. Even so the beating was most unpleasant and I think the entire class was glad when the lad did finally leave.

I expect I could have stayed on at school had I wanted but I did not. The purpose of it all had disappeared from my outlook. My brother had become interested in Theosophy and was introducing it to me. I was fascinated. It made immediate sense to my outlook. But it also seemed to make much conventional learning doubtful. What was the point of continuing with schooling when it was so distant from what really seemed to matter. It was time for school and me to part. But what was I to do? I was faced with the world of work but of what should my work consist? I had no idea. If I asked people I met or any one near me, I would receive answers such as "What is your bent?" "What are your interests?" "Where do you see yourself going?" To such questions my answer was always the same: "I don't know." I had no idea, yet it mattered enormously. I desperately wanted my work to be interesting. This constituted dilemma number 1.

Dilemma number 2 was conscription which was looming when I reached eighteen. That would be next year. Dilemma number 3 was mother. I had loved her so much and she still loved me. Yet by this time, I had tired of her closeness. It felt more like smothering than mothering and I wanted to be free of it all.

To sum up, my position was now this. I had ended up in a world which was exerting what seemed like considerable pressures on me. I wanted to be interested in my employment yet had no notion what I should do. Further, I hated the idea of military service in any form. The whole idea of killing people was most repulsive. Who could help me? Least of all mother - from whom I was pressing for release.

Yet before I answer these problems I need to consider the war, i.e. World War II, and how I was thinking about it.

Chapter Five

Life in the War

When war broke out in 1939, I was nine years old. The family was grouped around the radio when the Prime Minister made the necessary broadcast. We wondered what would happen but as the broadcast finished, an air-raid siren sounded. Fortunately, it proved to be a false alarm. However, although alarms were already in place, air-raid shelters were not. They had been issued and father got to work to install ours. He dug what seemed a mighty hole in the back garden. The structure was mainly metal with a door at the front. He sunk the sides half way in the soil and then cemented them in. It took him a week or two to complete.

A few weeks later, council workers arrived and declared that the job would have to be done again because it was not really secure. Anyhow, it was all dug up and re-positioned. Then earth was added to cover the top. This was partly for further defence and partly to prevent the metal shining in the moonlight thus possibly attracting a bomb. So within a few weeks of the declaration of war, we were all ready for air-raids.

Ours was an Anderson shelter, a little over six foot long and about four wide. These were the standard issue. But not everyone got one. Next door, our neighbour, Mr. Sharplin, was in a reserved occupation, which meant that he had to make his own shelter. And make it he did, concrete sides and base and metal top. The Chivers family took to sniggering at his efforts which we watched from a window. When he had made all the sections he had to heave it all the way to the end of the garden and then erect it. I guess he realised that his efforts afforded us entertainment because, once completed, he invited us in to have a look. It was far better than ours; we were put to shame.

It was not long before the air-raids started in earnest, especially at night. Each time the air-raid siren sounded, you were supposed to jump out of bed and run down to the shelter. You were not supposed to wait to get dressed. Take your clothes with you was the idea and get dressed in the shelter. But who wants to dash down to the shelter in the garden in the winter, particularly when we had little on. We did not have to shed pyjamas – neither my brother nor I possessed them. We just wore old shirts to bed. At first, like a lot of families, we obeyed the siren dutifully. But as time wore on and raids became nightly, we generally got dressed as quickly as we could and then ran to the shelter. Quite often we just stayed put in bed or would get up and watch the dog fights in the air. One could see the German bombers in formation as they headed on towards London, while German fighter aircraft tried to provide protection against British fighters. At the same time, anti-aircraft shells would explode around the formation.

Yet although the aircraft were attracted especially towards London, we had a share too and we got used to hearing the whistle of German bombs. The whistle was meant to induce fear. Certainly, it was disturbing. Yet in our family, it was really only mother who became very agitated. We (my brother and I) would forget about it during the day. I would be at school, while my brother was at a private college learning administrative skills. Father was mostly absent in the Navy. Bombs did land in the road where we lived and all around us but it was not the systematic wiping out of an area such as parts of the capital experienced.

Next day we often listened to the aircraft losses as they were announced on the radio. The enemy always seemed to lose a lot, while the British lost few. I used to marvel at how good our planes must be compared to 'theirs', or was it the British fighter pilots' skills? It was only some time after the war that I learned about control of news and information management. Then another illusion bit the dust.

There were, as might be expected, frequently more than one raid a night, often supplemented by more raids in the day. For the latter, there were school and college shelters. My brother assured me that when one bomb did land very close to our house I was blown out of bed. It seems I continued my slumbers on the floor till returned to bed by my mother.

For many a morning after a raid, my brother became keen on collecting shrapnel. Mother and her two sons would emerge from our house, one of whom (me) protesting about the cold. Mother insisted that the collecting operation had to be done before school. To leave it till after school, would mean that her two boys would be separated from her and therefore at risk on their own. She could not bear the thought of that. I took little part in the collecting activity but my brother was keen enough for the two of us. Not surprisingly he soon acquired quite a collection.

In general, I would assess my attitude to the war as one of no particular concern or interest. Yet there were one or two occasions when I was deeply affected. One of these was during 1940. I was still in the junior school. My form teacher was a Miss Paul of whom I was apprehensive because I knew that my brother had said she was a source of trouble. I had not been in this form long when mother said that her nerves were now so bad that the family would have to take a break and live with an aunt in Devon for a while. Father had not been 'called up' at this stage so he was not pleased to hear that mother planned to leave home – with her two boys of course. Her two boys were far from pleased either. It meant a break in our schooling and a possible transfer to a school in Devon. So my brother and I asked if we could stay put. But mother would not hear of it. She had to take her family with her. So we were transported by train to the aunt in Devon where we stayed for several months. No school transfer arrangements had been made; hence my brother and I simply used the time to go for walks and cycle rides. Eventually, mother decided that she was sufficiently rested to return to Romford. Therefore, back we came, and back to Miss Paul I had to go. I suspected that she would seize on my absence as a chance to belittle me. I was right! The very first day of my return, while the class was busy reading, she called me out to stand beside her desk. She wasted no time, but said that the whole form, bar me, had remained under the bombing but that I had let the form down by leaving. I protested that my brother and I had been taken by our mother even though we did not want to go. All this she ignored. How far the other children in the class heard any of this I have little idea. I was so indignant I did not notice. I did not tell either parent of his incident since I reckoned that if Miss Paul was challenged by my parents she would find further ways of degrading me. Later, someone told me that she (Miss Paul) had got married and I noticed that she seemed to mellow in her classroom behaviour. Even so, I loved her not, and even to this day find it difficult to forgive her in my heart. In child language, she just wanted to 'score' and she chose a child to do so since she knew he could not adequately 'fight back'.

A second incident in the war also proved to be unforgettable. This occurred towards the end of national hostilities, some time in 1944. I was going home for lunch one day and just about to leave the gates of the grammar school behind me when I heard what I thought was a lorry coming down the road. Trees blocked my vision of the road. Hence I could rely only on hearing. But when I reached the road I could see no lorry. Yet the sound was now deafening. Then I looked in the only direction I had not thought to consider – upwards. Perhaps fifty feet over my head was a German flying bomb. It barely missed the houses across the road as it proceeded on its way. This was the only time I experienced real fear during the war; I could feel my knees knocking. My brother had a similar narrow escape when He was just in time to leap to safety one day out of the way of a trailing cable of a run-away barrage balloon as it passed over our back garden.

I tell these stores to explain that neither my brother nor I were deeply affected by the war itself. But our experience was not that of some of the big cities where whole areas were wiped out. Our house was knocked about and, like many others, was subject to extensive repairs after hostilities were over. But we were never bombed out. The really heavy bombing was the experience of some areas, but not ours, while many rural areas knew no bombing at all. Comparing notes with persons who were children during the war shows that some were deeply affected. Some, like our mother, found the bombing terrifying. Others were injured by the bombing and these experiences stood out in their minds. However, for very many children, the war was not a deeply upsetting experience.

Food shortages did have some impact. Mother had coupons, which she used at the local co-operative retail store. But what she was able to purchase was limited since some food items had simply disappeared. Eggs in shells had been replaced by dried egg, which no matter what was done with it, never seemed to lose its powdery flavour. There was a very limited ration of meat supplemented by corned beef. Butter was strictly rationed so that most of the time the family had to make do with margarine. Cream vanished; milk and cheese were available in very limited quantities. Bananas existed only for special diets; they were unseen by most people till the war ended. Sweets were rationed and limited in form -- doubtless of benefit to our teeth. People knew that they were not eating well, even though they put up with it because of their commitment to the war effort. Such as I contacted morale, it seemed well enough. Probably, the radio played an important part in this. It offered some choice and, like most families, we followed particular programmes.

A further point worth noting is the effect of the war on political attitudes. When the war ended in 1945, Winston Churchill was prime-minister. His speeches in the war were legendary and he was accorded great esteem for his role in clarifying the situation in respect of Germany before hostilities broke out. Now with victory, many people expected him to sweep the Conservative Party to power. Yet it was the Labour Party which enjoyed election success. The war had produced a great social change. It had stimulated the realization of the importance of the British people. Not only had it brought people together around a sense of nationhood but it had stimulated new values concerning the need for welfare. There was a collective sense of selfhood which favoured the Labour Party and its goals of welfare for all.

How far did I as a 16/17 year old lad realize these changes? Not much I am sorry to say. There was no political conversation in the home. I recall that father was a Labour supporter but he was serving in the Navy and not present in the home for most of the war. At school, there was some discussion about the changes. But these would be passing remarks during a lesson on some subject and that subject was not about social change, even if the remark was.

I was still at school when my psychic experiences began. I think they are worth description.

Chapter Six

Psychic experiences

As a teenager I had a series of psychic experiences. But why bother to consider them here in an autobiography? Since I had challenged the religious teaching at school, I feel that it would be useful to explain that I did not subscribe to a crass form of materialism which argued that only the physical world existed. I have already explained my attraction to Theosophy as a teenager. It seemed that this elucidated so much which the religious teaching of the Church did not. A second reason for considering pychism is that it has a considerable following in so-called Spiritualism. However although I accept the existence of a vast world outside the physical I reject the notion that so-called spirit messages through mediums are spiritual. Rather are these messages the product of persons we knew in physical form. Such persons were no more specially spiritual than anyone else. It follows that they are no more likely to be spiritual when they pass over. However, my experiences do confirm the psychic world.

To explain the circumstances of my experience I need to hark back to myself as a boy somewhere between eight to ten years of age. For some reason grandmother, (i.e. mother's mother) was spending a few days with us in our house in Romford. She was accompanied by one of her sisters (an aunt to us brothers). Our mother, grandmother the aunt and I were all grouped around the fire in the living room. The aunt had a cold and was regularly using paper handkerchiefs. When used, she put these in the coal scuttle. Mother asked the aunt to desist. Grandmother supported this asking the old lady to use a pocket for the used hankies.

However, the old aunt just went on using the coal scuttle. So I kept on reporting the fact and mother and grandmother kept on telling the aunt to use her pocket. In the end mother signalled to me to be quiet. This I did but by that time I expect the aunt was peeved. She died a year or two later.

Now we have to come forward. I would have been about fourteen years old. One morning I found that my bedroom door would not open. After a number of unsuccessful attempts I gave up trying. A little later I tried again and found the door opened without any difficulty. I thought no more about it. But when the same problem recurred the next day and on subsequent days and at different times of the day, I realised that something untoward was happening. It could not be that my brother was holding the door handle from the other side of the door because on several occasions I could see him in the garden through the window. Could it be that the door handle needed replacement? After careful examination, I could find nothing wrong with it. Gradually I came to the conclusion that I was experiencing a psychic phenomenon. That was why I concluded that, it must be that the old aunt who had passed away, must be responsible. She was getting her own back, as we say.

As time progressed I found other doors in the house did not respond to me. But always it was when I was alone. I began to try reasoning with the psychic person. I would say, after wrestling with a door handle: "Now you have had your fun, please let me out." I usually had to wait a little while before she (if such it was) responded. This situation must have continued for several months. Perhaps strangely I was not frightened. Probably this was because I understood the situation. Then, as suddenly as it had started, it stopped, and I found no more difficulty with any of the door handles in the house. On a number of occasions I told my brother about the problem but he seemed disinterested. I expect he thought I was not too good at opening doors.

Nothing much more of a psychic nature occurred till I was in my late teens. I then went to one or two séances and also took part in some table tapping sessions. All of this was really to do with friends who were interested and wanted to experiment. At the séances there would be thirty to forty attendees, a number of whom received messages. These messages were mostly about relatives (deceased or living) of those present and were generally full of hope and comfort. The table tapping produced more dramatic results. It was definitely more eventful. Even though those present merely had their fingers lightly on it, the table bumped around to supply yes or no answers to questions. On a further occasion I was with others at an informal meeting. One of those present was receiving a message from "the other side". I became very drowsy and drifted off to sleep. I mention this because it was later explained to me by those present that my job had been to supply the power for the occasion. Later there were similar occasions when, though interested in the psychic activities I would drift off into slumber. So as I was not bored by events, I must assume that my proclivity for sleep was due to my readiness to supply power.

I take the view that psychism is useful because it helps to confirm that belief in the sole existence of a material world is nonsense. That which is outside the mundane is valuable since many people already know this (i.e. via experience) and are looking for confirmation to help them in discussions with others. Psychism among teenagers is said to be relatively common. I suggest that it is important not to overlook it as one gets older since it provides evidence of a world beyond the physical.

However, I must return to one of my dilemmas – leaving home.

Chapter Seven

Leaving Home

You may recall that this was one of my dilemmas - leaving home. I knew that I needed to put space between mother and myself. She had poured all her love onto my brother and me and lost interest in father, her husband. She had smothered us in love and watched over us with devoted care. Too much care; too much closeness; too much devotion. As children, we had benefited much from her love. It had helped to provide us with emotional stability and we responded by loving her. But she had forgotten to allow us to break free now we were teenagers. Yet both of us wanted independence. How could that be achieved?

For my brother the problem was not so great. He had a more outgoing personality than me. So he felt less confined than I did. In any case, he would be conscripted for military service once he was eighteen. In those days the age of majority was twenty-one. So at sixteen, I felt caged and unable to do anything about it. Mother would not willingly let me go and played the martyr at any such suggestion. Little did I know it but help was at hand.

I had just found my first job. Since I did not know what kind of work I wanted to do, I followed lamely in my father's footsteps and found clerical work in London. I was with Marshall's Food Products which meant travelling by train up to that great metropolis every week-day. At the same time as this was occurring another development was emerging of a more thoughtful kind. My brother who had long standing interests in mysticism had made contact with the Theosophical Society. Gradually, I joined him in his trips to the Society's London headquarters.

I found Theosophy fascinating. At school I had been asked to believe in a religious story which seemed to me then, and still does, as wish fulfilment: a personal God, the importance of this belief, the doctrine of Jesus Christ -- the Son of God. How could each of us have but one life when there were such enormous differences in life chances, romantic opportunities, the quality of male and female roles within some societies. But Theosophy offered a God within ourselves to be realised by us all during a great span of incarnations, our evolution spurred on by karma (cause and effect) until we learned to live unselfishly over many lives. Along with this went a cosmology which gave me an insight into life and an overall perspective with which to understand myself and the world as a whole.

Together, my brother and I formed a Theosophical youth group. One of the people who helped us in this respect was a middle aged friend, whom we invited to give us talks. This speaker had a philosophy of his own as well as a knowledge of occultism. He offered friendship but even more important to me was his counselling. It was this which explained my mother's possessive love and which provided me with a bastion of support. This I needed in order to withstand mother's incessant martyrdom. This enabled me to realise that I had reached the stage where the only answer was to make a complete break with home.

The middle aged friend offered his home as shelter, and we two lads were glad to accept. His name was Bancroft but later, after his father's death, he became known as the Count de Santi. He had had a difficult upbringing with a father, whose profession had dominated his interests and goals. The entire family was upper class in its identification and values, and this applied too, to the middle aged count whom we knew. He lived with a friend, Brian, a young man who earned a living in his father's photography business. The Count himself earned some money from his speaking engagements. Hfis background was that of an actor. His own home life had been hard when his irascible father threw him out of his house, and our friend (the Count) ended up on the embankment in London.

His current accommodation was in Pimlico in London. Nearby was Vauxhall Bridge, his downstairs flat being situated facing the Thames embankment. A Peabody Buildings, then converted into flats, stood across the road. Our friend's flat consisted of one living room, and two bedrooms. There was a passageway, joining the rooms, and serving the flat with a front door. At the end of the passage was a kitchen with a back door giving onto a small yard and outside lavatory. Up a flight of stairs there was a bathroom, which seemed to serve all the flats – a ground floor flat and another above. Brian had one of the bedrooms and the other served my brother and me. There was only one bed in this bedroom and most nights I had to sleep on the floor till my brother's 'call-up' arrived in a few weeks. So pleased was I to leave home, that my current accommodation constituted no problem. I used to wind myself into a flannelette sheet and pull a blanket over the top. Needless to say, the bedrooms had no heating. There was a coal fire in the living room but that was all.

Such was my accommodation for a little over a year. But since I was 16-17 at that time it may be wondered why mother did not seek to use the law to bring me back. But she did not. Instead, she turned her need for affection onto her husband. In her home, there was no one else to love. I have often marvelled over the fact that my leaving home brought my parents together. It was years later before I heard of this change -- when my brother made contact with our home.

What really mattered about my new home situation was the conversation. I could explore my mother's feelings towards me and mine towards her. This was enormously helpful to me. So were the lectures and group meetings at the Theosophical Society. When my brother joined the Army on Conscription I took over as secretary of the Theosophical Youth Group. Meetings also grew up around the Count in his flat. There were no more than five or six of us: Brian, Walter (whom we called Wally), my brother when he could join us and a couple of other young men. Two or three others would occasionally attend. After some months of meetings, several of us, including me, joined the Arcane School. This meant that our meetings were less likely to be based on readings from Blavatsky's *The Secret Doctrine* (Adyar Edition, 1938) and more likely to be based on Alice Bailey's *A Treatise on Cosmic Fire*, (London: Lucis Press, 1925).

By this time we had found out that the Count was a fourth degree initiate and that his master was Koot Hoomi, who was invariably referred to as K.H. The meetings were led by the Count but various advanced beings would often take over, delivering comments and points relating to discussions through the Count, who was dominated by them psychically. Persons wishing to know the style of conversation should read the works of the Tibetan, for example the two volumes of Alice Bailey's *Discipleship in the New Age*, (London: Lucis Press, 1944). Discussions would often take place at these meetings. Mostly, these did not generate much insight. Looking back, I would suggest that we should have made more effort to stimulate our thinking.

Gradually, it was borne in upon me that we were being 'initiated', one or two at a time. This applied to several of us but not others. However, the form of the initiation seemed to follow a pattern. One stripped naked and then the Count would touch each of the centres in turn. So far as I could discover the others who were 'initiated' registered no response. However, for me it was a powerful experience. Both elbows went numb when my throat was touched. I could feel power coursing through my body. When asked about this at the end of the 'ceremony' I was told that I would become a teacher. At that time, it did not mean a lot since I had no qualifications, formal or informal; I was still coasting along as a clerical worker.

Were we really initiated? Perhaps it was initiation 1. But I am unsure, especially since the others who had the same experience seemed to register so little. Maybe it was merely the introduction of some power to find out the nature of group members' spiritual development, if any.

Such was the situation when I reached 18 and promptly received my "call-up" papers. This issue brings me to another of my dilemmas. If I entered the armed forces I would have to be ready to take human life and I should be expected to be trained in how to do so. The idea was anathema to me. Fortunately the Count and most of the group were followers of non-violence and we had experienced many discussions on the subject. Hence I was all ready to make my case for conscientious objection. However it is no easy route. You need to work out some kind of philosophy of life, also some strategies for action for solving international disputes. All of which has to be done by a lad who is still fresh from school and who is still learning about work and employment, let alone world conflicts. Moreover you have to state your case before a tribunal and explain why you believe participation in war is fundamentally wrong. My tribunal consisted of three elderly men. The would-be conscientious objectors consisted of a handful of young men. Each of them proceeded into the dock to present their case individually. Each of them argued their case and then responded to questions from the tribunal, who also took account of a prepared statement from each applicant. I watched in horror as each applicant was turned down.

I was the last to make my case that morning. My brother spoke on my behalf. He had had a difficult route to conscientious objection. He had joined the army before giving serious thought to the issue. Like me he was a member of our group and, like me, converted to the philosophy of non-violence. He had to refuse orders while in uniform, which situation led to a spell in prison. In due course, he achieved recognition as a conscientious objector I should think his presence helped my case since it showed that I must have had plenty of opportunity to discuss the relevant issues. The result was that my case was accepted, the only one of the morning to be so. Why was I the successful one? Possible answers might be: my brother s help, my shining sincerity, or perhaps it was because it was getting late and lunch awaited a doubtless hungry tribunal. I was awarded two years conditional service, and followed my brother into hospital porter work.

It was Charing Cross Hospital. Not the current one but its predecessor. There lurked temptation – in the form of maids. Some of these were British but the majority were drawn from a large Italian contingent. Nearly all were young, nubile and alluring. Their approach to sexuality was to lead young men on, enjoy being fondled but not permit removal of clothing, still less sexual contact. That typified the era. Women had so much to lose if they failed to say 'no' at the necessary moment that this was what they said. True there were contraceptives but they were not readily obtainable, as they have long since become. They were available in men's hairdressers and some chemist shops stocked them. But they would have to be asked for in the hearing of everyone in the hairdressers or shop at the time. Would a lad's age be queried? Would any children present ask what a condom was? Would the hairdresser try to exploit the lad's embarrassment? It would be a brave teenager who dared to voice his wish for even careful sexual experience. I lacked any such courage. My guess is that contraceptives were also little available to unmarried women. Hence they saw to it that they remained on the conventionally acceptable side of sex expression.

Yet I doubt if I really wanted sexual experience. Physically I did; I knew that by this time. But I was less keen to be involved with the girls as young people. For me, their lifestyle was unattractive: light music, little by way of serious conversation. So, odd as it may seem, at least part of me was glad to be frustrated. The reason for this was the type of female that I was meeting. Later I met middle class girls. By that time I had made some advance educationally and unsurprisingly I found middle class girls much to my liking.

But to revert to the earlier stage, I was meeting young maids – their work title as well as their unmarried status. As indicated, they excelled at stimulating sexual arousal. Perhaps for this reason the type of sexual arousal which I developed at this time was to stay with me till quite late in my life. I must confess as to its immaturity. I was attracted to the physical form; for me, the psychological disposition of the female went largely unnoticed. I developed what I would characterise as a lascivious stare which I understand to be frightening to a number of females at a distance of several yards. Various women used to depart from my radius at some speed.

It was while we were living in Pimlico that we made a number of friends and acquaintances. They entered the lives of the group and the Count. For the most part I found their company acceptable, though I seldom entered the conversations which were largely led by the Count. One of the characters who joined us at Theosophical meetings was Reggie. Though the son of a wealthy Swiss businessman, he had been educated in Britain and sounded as British as the rest of us. He would often drop in on us during the evening and regale us with his various notions. He was intelligent, outstandingly extroverted, bursting with chatter, much of which concerned his deluded belief in his true love partner. We humoured him in this regard. Most of the time he seemed to see her from afar though he did once meet her – fleetingly it seemed. Perhaps he realised that you must not get too close to a dream in case it falls apart. On the plus side, he was friendly and had an entertaining aspect.

However, over time, the obsession with his paramour tended to pall. She, it seemed was ready to play Isolde to his Tristan. But where was Isolde? Yet none of our group sought to disillusion him. In the end, he stopped his visits to us and I think he must have returned to Switzerland.

A couple whom we also met via the Theosophical youth group, came to represent the ideal marriage, so far as I was concerned. To meet them entering or leaving the Theosophical headquarters would invariably find them walking hand in hand and ready to make conversation about some topic or other. One day I mentioned to another member of the youth group that I considered this couple to constitute an ideal marriage. He quickly disillusioned me. It seemed that she was at her wit's end with him and his shallow optimism in life. This was a lesson to me. Some people are well able to disguise their behaviour in terms of conventional norms. This wins such people status among their acquaintances. But one must probe a little deeper if one wishes to discover a more accurate perspective to a relationship.

Perhaps this is the point where it seems relevant to acknowledge that there were one or two members of the Theosophical Youth group who drifted off into deeper relationships. The group would see less of them in consequence. However, for the most part the group remained strong. Membership was largely based on questions. What sort of questions? Typical might be: Is there a purpose in life? Why am I here? Is there some kind of God? Is human nature evolving? And so on. Of course there are materialistic answers to such questions which became familiar to me later on. For example, do not questions of this nature reveal the wish to believe in mystical dreams? For my part, however, I would argue that they indicate the higher aspects of human nature. Mundane answers to philosophical issues are relevant because they reveal that the mundane does not suffice.

This phase of my life ended when the Count left Britain for France, taking several members of our small circle with him. These were persons who might be expected to get employment so that the group could gradually re-form. I was nearing eighteen and expecting call-up for national service, (as it was called), quite soon. I had no skills or higher education at this stage. So I remained in the Pimlico flat with two others of the group. In practice, we soon moved to another London flat close to Victoria Station. We kept going as a group for something over a year. We broke up gradually, I being the first to depart.

Before leaving this chapter it would seem relevant to consider the philosophical nature of the group. It was this philosophy around which the group revolved. It was why we were a group. I have already mentioned some of the Theosophical literature. In the last few months, before the Count's departure, we had found the Alice Bailey literature and had joined the Arcane School. These various sources provided us with answers to many of the kind of questions mentioned a little earlier. It told us where we came from and how we had evolved. But it also expected a particular way of life based on brotherhood. This was immensely useful for it meant that future development lay in a group orientation rather than in individualism. All this is to be explored in due course. Right now, I must continue my story, turning back to the issue of employment.

Chapter Eight

Nurse or Goaler?

To begin with I pick up on two phases of my life. The first concerns my two years of compulsory hospital service. The second phase might be regarded as the more important since it was my choice, an early attempt to answer the third dilemma: what work should I do in life? In this regard, metaphor will be found to play an important part, as is apparent in the chapter title. Metaphor stimulates thought. One can detach oneself from the daily round and take a look at what happened from a detached perspective, considering matters reflectively rather than as a person pushed into response to everyday eventualities.

It will be recalled that I had left school wanting to find interesting work yet little able to determine what that might be. My answer had been to follow in my father's footsteps and become a clerk. The work was far from interesting and perhaps for this reason I can remember little of what I actually did. I was not particularly bothered about the situation since, as a lad of seventeen, I knew that I should have to make some important decisions when 'call-up' came in a year's time. So I settled down to a bored spell of 'pen-pushing in Marshall's Food Products, the employer. The employees consisted of two or three dozen men and women who occupied a floor of a building, reasonably close to Liverpool Street Station which was my point of arrival in London and departure later in the day. The employees did not seem to be particularly interested in each other, though the younger women would go off into huddles to discuss their boy-friends. More prominent was a young man who declared his homosexuality adding that he was very much available to any of the male staff who might be interested. During this era, homosexuality was still taboo. Hence his openness in respect of the subject won him no more than some degree of disdain. Speaking for myself, I found the entire subject embarrassing. I had made no contact with it, either at home or at school.

There was scarcely time to celebrate my eighteenth birthday before my 'call-up' papers arrived. It was 1948 and I was living in the Pimlico flat with the small group around the Count. It will be recalled that my conscientious objection had been accepted, conditional on two years' hospital service. I spent my time in the dispensary of Charing Cross Hospital. I was a porter and work consisted of bottle washing humping huge bales of materials to the store and general cleaning and clearing jobs.

The staff were few yet a fair cross-section of humanity. In charge was the head pharmacist, whom we called Lips because his prominent lips were pursed up by nature into a permanent pucker. He was a kind man but somewhat aloof. His second in command was friendly yet seemed a little crude in thought and speech. There were five other pharmacists – three male and two female. One of the latter, middle-aged and single, liked to play a girlish role with one of the older male pharmacists, who was, in fact, married. However, she was of no special importance to him. His eyes were set on one of the ladies in hospital reception. While I delivered most of the prescriptions all over the hospital, he delivered the ones to reception. No one wondered why!

The chap who was my immediate boss was someone called Arthur, a jocular working class middle-aged male. He was a porter like me. The other male pharmacist was a young man of around thirty. He was tall with a slouching, curious walk. He was interested in all kind of things and could converse intelligently on a wide variety of subjects. However, he was in some ways immature and psychologically maladjusted. So one had to watch what one said to him or he would become childishly upset. The remaining lady pharmacist was around middle age. She was efficient but quite often not present due to gynaecological treatment. But, like the others, she was pleasant enough so that I passed two reasonably happy years till my papers came confirming my release from conditional service. I can remember little more about the pharmacy since my work was of no interest. My focus was the group back at the Count's flat, where we had many interesting discussions.

My work dilemma was still dominant. Yet I had no idea what kind of work I should seek. Discussion with group members turned my attention towards psychiatric nursing. That would be socially useful and I felt the subject to be important. I was too, interested in mental health though I could claim no special psychological knowledge. However, it was worth a try. It was not long before I found myself a trainee mental nurse in the Bethlam Royal Hospital in Kent. It was the early 1950s and I was in my early twenties.

This was scarcely more than an episode in my life but it is worthy of careful consideration because it is such an important occupation in a crucial profession. Regularly I read of the growth of mental illness and how it must be accorded prominence and funding. I intend to analyse my experience of it via the metaphor *Cross Purposes*. Why? Because I believe this to have been a reasonable description of the so-called hospital treatment. Let me start with my expectations of mental nursing. Often when one asks people about their expectations of some circumstance they reply that they had none. But of course they did; we all do. We do not recognise these expectations because they are so much part of our general socialisation plus, perhaps our half formulated wishes. This was the form of my expectations. I expected that in some way, I should be able to play a part, albeit a minor one, in the treatment of patients.

The initial nurse training came as something of a shock. You were made to realise quickly that rules and regulations were to receive pride of place in your work life. Moreover nurse tutors were to be treated with no little respect. I suppose the same applied to the doctors (or psychiatrists) though I saw little of them. In fact, only one played any part in my practice – for a discussion on ward patients. The clergy were a little more in evidence. Much of the training period was spent on the ward where one became part of the staff, doing whatever was required. There were also lectures by the nurse tutors and a certain amount of writing. This was largely related to the lectures.

I was none too pleased with the living accommodation. The problem was that I had to share with two other young men, who were, like me, trainee mental nurses. One of these two was not long out of the Navy and we got on well enough. The other chap was perhaps in his late thirties. A Welshman, he was fond of trying out his tenor voice. He was ebullient and never tired of telling us about his activities, representative of the popular culture of the day. Visits to cinemas, cafes, dance halls, etc. On one occasion, he went to some kind of activity where he was able to meet film and television stars of the day, and we heard about this for some days afterwards. His taste and mine were distinct and I feel bound to say that he was, for me, someone to put up with. Towards the close of the initial introductory period I think he must have been in two minds whether to continue or drop out. I guess this may have been why one of the tutors explained that this chap had taken up mental nursing in order to help him understand his own mental problems which manifested as some lack of confidence. I do not think she would have raised such an issue unless he was considering leaving. I found this information helpful because it clarified his somewhat loud and boisterous manner, and afforded me the chance to achieve a more sympathetic view of him.

During my training period, I was assigned to a ward full of young lads, who must have ranged from their early to late teens, some even into their twenties. The case notes were available for the nurses to read and these covered occurrences on the ward as well as information on the lads' backgrounds. I gained the impression that the lads had been recommended for hospital treatment by various medical personnel. My own activity largely consisted in patrolling the ward, which I should think consisted of around twenty-five young men, i.e. the lads. I had to stop large groups forming since they could have then been in a position to force a break-out. Small groups were acceptable. However, it seemed that the lads were little interested in friendship. Just one or two appeared to give some time to friendly association, and that was with a nurse, not another lad. Keeping an eye on the lads was not particularly easy because the ward was quite large: a dormitory, some single bedrooms, recreation rooms containing equipment, a kitchen and dining facilities.

At other times, I would be assigned the task of watching over just one lad. One of these was a lad on his own who appeared to have descended into a well of bitterness because his mother had remarried. Hence, it seemed, she no longer gave him pride of place in her attentions. Very possibly there was more to the case than what I saw while I observed him during a parental visit. However, other nurses certainly confirmed the nature of the problem. I noticed that he spoke with great attention to his mother. However, he was clearly not satisfied with her response. Once she was gone, he would revert to his daily routine: finger writing on the table in his bedroom. This he would do by the hour, indicating to me that he had no wish for conversation. Not surprisingly, observation in silence was a tedious task.

On occasion the psychiatrist would visit and this would usually end with a case conference in which the nurses reported on the activities of the patients over recent weeks. The charge nurse conducted proceedings and the psychiatrist might ask questions or respond to the nurses' reports. The few conferences I attended were silent affairs. Usually there was little or nothing to report. The nurses could ask question if they wanted or make observations and the psychiatrist would respond. But usually nobody said anything; silence reigned. However, I do recall my raising some line of activity which might be tried with one of the lads. The psychiatrist argued that it was immensely difficult to gain any response from the lads. I suspect that this was true enough but if so, the case conference idea was something of a mockery. There seemed to be no discussion, nor were the nurses asked to do anything other than observe. Few of the lads entered into discussion with the nurses or each other.

What the treatment consisted of was never discussed. The psychiatry might have been Freudian or at least semi-Freudian since Freud was still an important name in respect of treatment at that time, even if today there are more perspectives. However, academic psychology, was undergoing something of a rethink, led by the controversial figure of Hans Eysenck, (London: *The Uses and Abuses of Psychology*, Penguin Books, 1953. *Decline and Fall of the Freudian Empire*, Scott-Townsend, 1985) with his debunking of the 'master' which attracted much public attention. But let me stay with the treatment of the era. There were some drugs but not the ones which became important later. There was electric shock treatment which was often referred to as E.C.T. This was popular then, as it still is. There was lobotomy, cutting some nerves in the head. Doubtless there were other physical treatments of which I was ignorant.

What then was the dominant ethos of the ward? I am sorry to say, that so far as I could see it was containment. This operated in several ways. First of all there was the locked door policy on the ward. This may seem strange since patients were voluntary. However, the word voluntary needs assessment. Patients would have consented to hospitalisation but alternative options may have been far from desirable: remain at home with relatives becoming restless with the lad's mental condition, or some seemingly isolating condition like a hostel, or else some kind of custodial accommodation if a crime had been involved. Whatever the options, once in the mental hospital, there was no easy way out. Other wards seemed to have the same policy so far as I could tell and I rapidly became used to carrying a hefty bunch of keys wherever I went.

Another aspect of containment was the way patients were brought into line with staff requirements. Most of the time the lads were not compelled to do anything. They could go to occupational therapy or refuse, go to the recreation room or no, talk to another lad or a member of staff. There were a few requirements of patients: such as make their beds, or take their medicines. In practice, they were often inclined to be awkward. I think that the reason was that they saw this as a form of protest. The custodial situation was little to their liking so they tended to see themselves as resisting the regime.

My answer was to leave them alone. To intervene in any forceful way would have been a breach of acceptable behaviour and risk reprimand, even dismissal. However, 'leaving them alone' was not as simple as it sounds. Visualise a situation where only two members of staff are on duty when a dispute arises among the lads while another is refusing his medicine and yet another is claiming a headache for which he wants medicine. How can the staff serve all these situations at once? In addition there were -- the rules. They could be difficult to operate. Of course the lads were well aware of this and could devise ways of seeing that the rules were by no means easy to maintain.

A further form of containment consisted of the charge nurse. He was a stockily built, rotund man whose dominant intention seemed to be to let all the lads know that he could deal with any of them, i.e. physically overcome them. For the most part, I think he could. However, I heard of one occasion when one of the larger lads was showing resistance and the charge nurse had to call on another male nurse for help.

One might summarise the hospital organisation as follows. The ostensible goal was treatment. But such treatment as there was, was long term – often a matter of years. Whether or how far it was successful would be a matter for debate. In the short term, such help as could be rendered the patients was limited, even non-existent. The real day-to-day life of the ward was about keeping the patients away from society so that society could get on with its daily round uninterrupted by the mentally sick. Inevitably this meant that the nurses were also involved in the containment objective, e.g. the locked doors, preventing large groups of the lads from forming, requiring the taking of medicine.

What occurred to upset this situation related to gender. Duties on the lads' ward were shared by male and female nurses. The role was the same for both sexes. However, we were all in our twenties and thirties and this meant that there as a certain interest between the sexes. One or two of the female nurses liked the male nurses to demonstrate their masculinity. The chance to do this arose one day when a powerfully built male nurse decided to move an obstreperous lad. This was done by picking up the lad and taking him bodily to where the nurse wanted him to be. Needless to say, touching patients is a breach of the rules. But one of the female nurses was very taken by the action and advised me to adopt the same approach.

Here was a dilemma. A number of the lads were well built. They could have resisted any physical action. Hence wisdom suggested that any bodily action by a nurse involving the lads would be unwise. However, the suggestion of physical control with its aura of masculine prowess behind it was tempting. Moreover, not to adopt physical control risked being seen by the female nurses as lacking in the male role.

How should I respond the next time a lad did not do as asked? Several of the female nurses favoured physical coercion by the male nurses since they (the female nurses) felt that this would set the tone of obedience to the nurses' wishes in general. At the same time, I was increasingly coming to realise that physical coercion was a definite element in the operation of the ward. I also realised that the charge nurse covertly adopted such a policy. The ward was several flights off the ground and he was for ever glancing out of the window in case matron was paying us a casual visit. This helped to clarify the situation for me. Whatever the female nurses' perspective of the male nurses' role, I would play no part in physical coercion.

Yet this decision was not as simple as I thought. One day I was carrying out my usual watching brief on the ward when the alarm bell rang and a light on the indicator identified a particular ward as in need of immediate assistance. The drill for this situation was that you stopped whatever you were doing, left your ward, locking it behind you and make your way as quickly as possible to the ward needing help. When I arrived, the female charge nurse of this ward grabbed my glasses and directed me to a room where a powerfully built man, perhaps in his late thirties was threatening violence. He was lying in bed but his torso and arms were free. The charge nurse of the lads' ward was astride the patient's chest. A struggle was ensuing.

"I could break your arm," said the charge nurse of the lads' ward. His recourse to physical power was revealed in such situations.

"Then go on, do it," said the muscular patient.

He had, it seemed, cut up rough while resisting his medicine. The problem was short-lived because while he was being held the nurses could get a shot of dope into him. So the episode ended with the charge nurse of the patient's ward declaring that women might not continue much longer in mental hospitals. The charge nurse of the lads' ward accompanied by me returned to our own ward. My reason for recounting the episode is to expose once again the underlying element of physical control within the hospital. Of course, constraint in various forms underlies the day-to-day functioning of various organisations, and it may well be that the public see mental hospitals in these terms. However, it is not the type of orientation that one wishes to encourage. Employees in these hospitals aspire to an orientation of care. No doubt there will be occasions when a difficult mental patient will need to be calmed and sometimes this will require a medicine to foster slumber. However, in my view, where a patient refuses such medicine, his wishes should be respected. Perhaps I should add that in general terms, most mental hospital patients are no more violent than the public at large.

This illustration serves again the underlying element of physical power characterising mental hospitals at that time. I must confess that I know not how they have changed since the 1950s. However, media treatment of the subject makes it clear that mental ill-health is still the poor man of the health service. Thus *The Guardian* reported (14.08.2014) that "less than a third of people with common mental health problems get any treatment at all". Such was the view of the incoming president of the Royal College of Psychiatrists in Britain.

I was gradually coming to a conclusion. The nature of the work was little to my liking. Patrolling the ward was tedious. Then there was the general nursing instruction which was perhaps useful but had no interest for me. Again, there were the expectations of some of the nurses favouring physical methods of solving the lads' unwillingness to accept regulated behaviour. Worst of all was the general aura of containment within the ward. Should I try to stick it out or should I leave? But if I quit, I should be back with the problem of what work I should do. This dilemma was proving the most difficult of all!

Finally, I made up my mind to leave. A phobia helped me to make the decision. The subject of blood would lead me to pass out. This I duly did during one of the general nursing lectures. I did not explain the cause and the staff did not grasp the problem. Later on I had to overcome the phobia when, due to a diagnosis of anaemia I was proscribed iron tablets. In practice, this was to last for years and was accompanied by blood tests to find out if the anaemia was disappearing. Regular blood tests did the trick in that I had to make the necessary effort to accept the sight and discussion of blood without a qualm.

What had mental nursing to do with the metaphor cross-purposes? Let me explain. The aim of mental nursing was and still is to offer treatment to the mentally ill. The surrounding context of containment was no treatment. Indeed, I could see little that amounted to treatment. I expect the psychiatrists did their best but this appeared infrequent. In practice; I never saw a lad being asked to take part in a session with a psychiatrist. The physical treatments such as E.C.T. and lobotomy were carried out in a few cases. Whether these led to gradual, long-term change I know not. The drugs seemed to be the most promising but my stay was too short (six months) to pass any real judgment. Cross purposes sums up what I saw. Mental hospitals were intended to offer treatment but their performance seemed to me little likely to improve mental health. Rather was their health improvement intention undone by their actual performance. One must have some sympathy with the decision of the powers that be to reduce the number of these hospitals even if -- the alternative -- treatment in the community was so inadequately developed.

Since I have been critical of my mental hospital experience I feel the need to assess my views with such care as I can muster. Present methods of psychiatric treatment are showing signs of some development. But the methods I have mentioned do not seem promising to me. I believe that the time has come to try the methods advocated in Alice Bailey's *Esoteric Healing,* London: Lucis Press, 1953. However, its author acknowledges the difficulties involved. Even so, why not explore a trial and error approach, using the techniques and perspectives there advocated.

The approach advocates substitution, replacing the negative feeling with one in line with soul recognition. So if you are feeling jealousy or frustration, or aversion, etc. to persons around you, substitute a sense which is in line with the soul, such as love, purposefulness, kindness, etc. For example, if a particular person induces a sense of dislike, you could substitute a sense of interest in him/her, or love, or tolerance, etc. You are thus replacing negativity with a positive outlook. You are mastering your feelings and turning them into outlooks which are useful to you because you are the master of the situation. This is among the methods advocated by the Tibetan.* By following them you remain in control and this is a basic step towards freedom from the influence of personality. Instead you are following the path which leads to soul awareness.

Should I quit mental nursing, and if did, what should I do?

---

* For example Alice Bailey *The Light of the Soul*, 140, Lucis Press, 1989; and more in *Glamour A World Problem*, Lucis Pess, 1973.

Chapter Nine

From Heat to Light

Let me resume the consideration of my occupational activities. I was still living in London with my two friends. I gave up my role of hospital porter once my term of alternative service (alternative to the armed forces) was over. But the flat had to be paid for. However, I was unemployed and temporarily without an income. So I had to find work even though I still had no idea what I should do that would interest me. Hence my work role became the focus of conversation in the flat. Eventually a consensus emerged. Our diet was not good since none of us could cook. Hence that was the skill to learn. I was not convinced but the idea did make sense.

I got a job in the Ritz Hotel in London's Piccadilly. As a *commis* chef (learner) I started at 8 a.m. and finished at 6 p.m. with two hours free from 2 p.m. to 4 p.m. This split duty, as it was called, typified the trade at the time. Theirs (the chefs) was a lifestyle of carousal—not for the likes of a new boy like me. How then should I spend the two hours? There was not time to take the bus back to the Pimlico flat, nor could I really join the chefs who repaired to local cafes. All I could do was mooch aimlessly round London's West End and take note of the expensive lifestyle which I could not possibly afford.

To explain my work in this top class catering trade, I must set the scene. The kitchens of this trade were divided into *parties (sections)*. Each of these carried out a specific role. I was assigned to the sauce *partie*, which included all the roast work, in addition to the sauces. Next to this was the fish *partie*, while on the other side was the breakfast *partie* and next to that the vegetable *partie*. Outside the main kitchen was a bakery and next to that was the larder. In charge of each *partie* was a specialist chef. Other staff included porters and a *plongeur* who cleaned all the pans after soaking them in water. Over all this was the head chef, M. Avignon, at that time (1950s) and his *sous* chef (deputy).

At times of service, waiters would enter the kitchen and file down in front of the hotplate and *bain-marie*, from which the food was served. The hot plate is a heated metal surface with drawers below the top where prepared food could be kept warm and plated meals could be served. The *bain-marie* is a heated shallow water trough for holding prepared food items which needed a steamy atmosphere. As the waiters filed up to the head chef; they passed him their order slips, which he read out. Each *partie* then shouted out any items which were needed to complete the meal. For example, the *partie* where I was stationed would often have to yell to the larder staff for particular cuts of meat. All this took place in French, though the chefs themselves constituted a range of nationalities. In my day, around half the chefs were drawn from all over the British Isles. The kitchen language is special because it is not current French. It would be a Nineteenth Century version because that is when the top class restaurant trade grew up all over Europe.

When in the changing room, the behaviour of the chefs was childish to say the least. For example, they would play a game based on who could fart the loudest. Part of the reason for this may have been to conceal embarrassment in showing their underwear. On duty, in the kitchen, their behaviour was different. Pressures are such that there is little opportunity for time-wasting. Moreover, for much of the time, there was a degree of overall supervision, mostly from the *sous chef*.

But let me return to the kitchen itself. *Parties* consist of a bank of stoves set side by side in a line. The stoves were built of heavy metal and, at that time, burned coal. The tops consisted of concentric rings of metal which could be pulled away to reveal the glowing coals beneath. So far as I could see, many of these stoves were never allowed to go out. The first job of many of the staff on the morning shift was to bank up the stoves. When I first set foot in the kitchen it was pleasantly warm. I was clad in a chef's cotton jacket and trousers, which, apart from underpants and shoes was all I wore. Within an hour of starting, my entire clothing was soaked through with perspiration. Yet the kitchen became hotter and hotter. Well before lunch-time, the perspiration was coursing down the outside of my uniform since the clothing was too sodden to absorb any more. Much of the perspiration ended up in my shoes, which needed to be tight-fitting to prevent them slipping off.

One of my jobs was to keep the stoves continuously red hot – which meant topping up from time-to-time. This could only be done by exposing their red hot interiors. In addition, I would chop garlic or parsley and keep a large cauldron of brown sauce topped up with its ingredients. I was, too, often sent on errands, fetching pans, fetching cream from the larder (with which to top up some sauces), finding plates for silver service and so on. For these jobs, I was supposed to walk as quickly as possible. Running was forbidden because of the danger of collisions. In practice, like all the other lackeys, I ran.

By lunch-time, all the stoves on all the *parties* glowed red hot. The air was stifling; I guess the temperature to be in the thirties, even forties, Celsius. Yet it must have been even hotter for the chefs bent over the stoves as they prepared dishes. Thus the kitchen of the *haute cuisine* restaurant trade at that time, was an inferno, yet executing orders with military precision, requiring total attention. This latter was necessary since there were various tasks to keep track of - catching the orders as they were announced, noting the items called for by one's own *partie* (as that would affect which sauce would be required), watching and topping up the various sauces on the stove, ensuring there was enough of the garnishes and so on. But attention to all this had the rival of noise - the clatter of pans, the shouted orders, the crackle of grilled food under the salamander grill.

Suddenly, just after 2 p.m., the frenzy ceased. The leading chefs gathered together in a small ante-room and ate their meal, which so far as I could see, looked very tempting. Other less important chefs simply leaned up against a table within their *partie* as they consumed their meal, made up from items they had been preparing, while skivvies like me, looked askance at chicken bones with skin in a watery sauce. There was no point in bothering with that, so it was back to the changing room and out into the cold, wet air of a London winter, straight from kitchen conditions, hotter than the top heat of a Turkish bath.

When I finally knocked off for the day, around 6 p.m., I would fall asleep on the bus back to Pimlico. Luckily our flat was close to the bus terminus, or I should have ended up I know not where. When I got home, I would slump into a chair while my flat mates plied me with tea. Not that I could ever finish it before sleep took over. In all my life, before or since, I have never been so drained of energy. It was all I could do to drag myself to bed before sleep took over, uninterrupted until the alarm went off around 6 a.m. to wake me for another round of the same.

In my day, in the commercial trade, nearly all the chefs/cooks were male. It was a male culture too: drinking, swearing and being childish in a constant attempt to show off in some way. I stuck it for six months. In the meantime, my friends were discussing the situation. Our aim had been for me to learn to cook so that at least one of us could prepare meals to a good standard. The trouble was that I was too exhausted when I reached home to be able to do anything. A more sensible way for me to learn cooking would be for me to find a less enervating job which left me free for evening study. So I moved into hospital catering and took a one-year City and Guilds course in trade cooking at which I was successful.

I was now employed again at Charing Cross Hospital but this time as a cook or chef. At some stage I moved into the St. Thomas' Hospital group and was given charge of a small hospital for women situated between Westminster and Waterloo Bridges. The situation was rather prim and proper, with a deputy matron who was polite but also straight-laced. A new matron was appointed soon after I arrived and she seemed to me to epitomise much that was best about nursing: gentle and kindly. Hence for around two years all went well.

I was in charge of a couple of female cooks, who were undergoing the Institutional Management Association course (IMA). Relations between us varied. The *young ladies* had internalised a value system which meant that they saw themselves as exactly that. This could lead to somewhat strained relations at times since I found their stance a little too prudish and superior. However, for the most part we avoided quarrels.

Moreover, one of the young ladies was a German who had been in England long enough to speak excellent English. Unfortunately I found her very attractive and this exacerbated the situation since she was little enamoured of me. Looking back, I would count myself very lucky since, had she responded at all, we should quickly have entered a relationship to which I had given no thought at all. There were a number of maids at this hospital and I recall becoming enamoured of them too and in an equally superficial manner. But they largely retained their distance – which was just as well.

In hospitals, the cooking was carried out by both males and females which contrasted with the top class hotel and restaurant trade. The cooking there was male dominated. During my time at the Ritz there was just one female cook; she was based in the larder. How can this situation be explained? Male values were still in command in the work sphere, despite two world wars which had brought women more prominently into the work sector. But with the end of World War II, men returned home and re-asserted their claim to the world of work. Women took their place again in the home, caring for husband and children. But the influence of the wars had helped to provide women with more work opportunity and to some extent broadened their outlook to encompass commanding positions of a social and parliamentary nature. Patriarchy had not died but it had been weakened.

After a couple of years at the women's hospital, I wanted to move on and made the mistake of succumbing to the blandishments of a catering officer in a different hospital group. His kitchen was little enough but he painted a picture of what it was going to be and I fell for the mirage. Of course, in time, his vision might have become reality. But I had no wish to wait so long. Unwisely I gave notice and was unemployed for several weeks.

Since I had to have an income while I sought another job, I applied for a job selling soap on behalf of the blind. This must have been about the only time in my life that I have been involved in selling as a livelihood and I found it a daunting experience. I had to pick up my soap allocation from a chap who organised a number of salesmen. He was an entrepreneurial type. "Plug the line that it is for charity," was his refrain. It was just as well that a charity was involved because I could not help feeling that he would have invented one if there not been.

He would pick up his salesmen, including me, by car, bringing us all together so that the allocation procedure could be carried out at the same time as providing administrative briefings. Several of these salesmen used their cars in the selling process. They were allowed to charge for their use of petrol during this activity. This bothered the organiser no end. "How do I know that they are charging me only for trips selling soap?" Yet the sums involved must have been minuscule.

One Sunday afternoon, this organiser, accompanied by his wife witnessed me at full throttle speaking at Hyde Park Corner on behalf of nuclear disarmament – an activity I carried out for a couple of years. The following day, on collecting my soap allocation, he conveyed the idea that he found me an impressive speaker. However, I suspect that he reasoned that such a speaker should be a good soap salesman.

Not long after this I was out on my rounds in a none too salubrious area. My sales were not going well and I had just had a refusal from a chap who appeared quite disinterested in my peroration. I moved on down the road and looked up to find the disinterested chap I had just been talking to. He asked me to return for a moment, showing me into a tatty drawing room. I wondered if this was a pending sale. There were two men in the room, both in their thirties. They seemed impressed with me

> "You've got the right approach," said one.
> "And an honest face," said the other. "We could make a business out of this."
> "Is this going to improve my sales?" I queried. I suppose I should be considered simply naïve!

Yet even as I spoke I noticed that they were sizing up my potential as a salesman and that their perspective was that the three of us might form a sales team. Their idea was that the three of us team up as crooks. One of them took some convincing that I saw the proposition as morally unacceptable! Soon after this, I joined the editorial staff of Peace News, the pacifist newspaper.

The pacifist movement was changing at this time. It had been closely related to the old idea enshrined in the Peace Pledge Union. This was an organisation based on the idea of seeking signatures for a peace pledge which committed the signatory to refuse to take part in war. It was relevant to the inter-war era idea. But was it still relevant by the World War II era? The nuclear disarmament movement offered an opportunity for updating the idea of resisting the very worst which war could bring – mass slaughter. The movement for peace had been revived. Hugh Brock, the editor of Peace News at that time, saw the potential in the movement and asked an expert in semaphore to come up with an idea around which the movement against nuclear weapons could unite. That was how the three-spoke wheel of the campaign came about.

There was an infectious feeling that a widespread ban on nuclear weapons might be possible since it was felt that one or more countries could give the lead. Nuclear war otherwise seemed likely, perhaps inevitable in the end, since the conflagration could come about by intention or accident. The intention was on the agenda on occasion, while accidents involving nuclear weapons continued to occur. At Peace News I became sub-editor and remained at this post for several years. It was not a particularly interesting job but it did carry a fair amount of responsibility.

The role of the sub-editor is to lay out the newspaper. That means arranging the items on the pages. Another job was to think up headlines and a further task is to read over the copy, which means scanning the printed stories in order to remove errors. In these respects, I was something of a disaster. I had never been a good speller and I should acknowledge more errors than I care to remember. The pay was hopeless as can be imagined. Fortunately, I needed only enough to cover food and rent. Copies were sold by dedicated sales-personnel but most copies were destined for committed readers/purchasers. We produced around 8,000 copies a week while I was in post and this enabled a small staff to maintain the newspaper.

I was at the heart of a movement in which I believed, though I always harboured one doubt – of which more anon. For the moment, let me examine two important developments which were to have much influence on my life. The first of these was my marriage in

1957. The second was the commencement of part-time degree study the following year. For some time, I had been seeking someone to love. We both seemed in need of a partner and became a pair of love birds for several months before tying the knot. Since I had no time for the Church, it was a Registry Office affair. My wife's parents attended but I preferred not to invite mine.

Around this time I began public speaking appearances at Hyde Park Corner. My subject was nuclear disarmament and I had no difficulty attracting a good crowd. I kept this going for about a year and a half to two years. I had a practical problem. To talk to a crowd, you need a platform in order for your voice to be heard by the listeners at a distance. I had a platform though I cannot remember where I got it. However, by this time the group, which included me had moved to the Victoria area of London. So I was faced with the need of transporting my platform to Hyde Park Corner.

Faced with the problem of finding somewhere to store the platform I found a nearby basement. It looked like a block of flats but there seemed to be no one of whom to make enquiries. So I stored the platform in a convenient basement alcove. Every Sunday from then on I would collect the platform and carry it the few yards to Speakers' Corner. For some weeks, all went well. Then catastrophe! Returning from the Corner I proceeded to the basement as usual, where I stowed the platform. I then ascended to street level where my wife, who was with me, exclaimed "You're entirely green!" Between collecting the platform and returning it, the basement had been painted, leaving me resembling a puny version of the Incredible Hulk. There was nothing for it but the removal of all my outer garments and then return home (to Ealing, since marriage). As best I recall, from then onwards I took the platform with me every Sunday on the Underground train service. Apparently, there is a film of me in full spate at Speakers' Corner. It forms part of a video about the British nuclear disarmament movement at that time. It has been shown in a number of contexts in various countries, though I have not myself seen it.

The Campaign for Nuclear Disarmament (CND) was now the dominant organisation in the peace movement and this held various campaigns, speeches and marches. The principal section of CND was vigorous in its campaigning but law-abiding nonetheless. But a small section of CND engaged in civil disobedience in order to attract attention to the nuclear disarmament case. My wish to join the civil disobedience activities did not have my wife's support and I felt unable to risk the break-up of my marriage. However, I should have had the courage of my convictions and must accept the minor role that I played in civil disobedience as evidence of my personal inadequacy. Eventually, I did become involved in a large scale demonstration against nuclear weapons. It consisted of a march which closed with a mass rally in Trafalgar Square in London. It had been declared illegal so arrests were large-scale. In court I refused to pay the fine and was jailed for a week in Brixton Prison.

As an experience it was interesting. I found that the principal problem was the sheer boredom of life there. The morning begins with slopping out. This is followed by breakfast and then some work, which consisted of sewing mailbags. Exercise in the prison yard was then organised with inmates strung out in a 'crocodile' formation. That way no one was beside you which would have encouraged conversation – that being forbidden. The greater part of one's time was spent in the prison cells chatting. There were two of us in my cell and in 'free time' we could meet up with one or two others, also from the demonstration.

To outsiders, this might sound quite acceptable. However, conditions were primitive. All washing was in cold water and I never saw a bath during my period of captivity. I did see some sparkling new showers but never did I see them in use. My guess is that their principal function was for the governor to be able to show them off whenever he took a visiting party round.

About a year after my marriage, I wanted to leave Peace News because I was seeking a better income. Moreover, I felt unable to pursue an adequate role in the developing civil disobedience, as I was too committed to my wife to be willing to risk a lengthy prison sentence. I had also begun part-time study for a sociology degree since I felt I needed better to understand the world around me. An important source of stimulation for this was the fact that I found myself considered intellectually inadequate by other members of the peace movement around me.

Hence I needed a job which would leave me free in the evenings to do study. Some kind of clerical work seemed appropriate and an occupation with career possibilities would be attractive. These views led me towards an application to the London County Council where I was offered a clerical position at County Hall, Westminster. Here I spent two years in the education department while the LCC changed into the GLC—the Greater London Council. By that time I was aged 32.

My job consisted of an examination of staff returns from London schools. These returns noted teachers' absences, which information I had to transfer onto a card filing system, which was used to advise the salaries' section on pay variations, deductions, etc. The work was thoroughly tedious.

When I had completed two years I sat the examination for the administrative grade and was successful. This opened the way to a year's training, consisting mainly of movement around a number of the Council's departments, many of which were outside County Hall. The training period was useful to me because the work was participatory and observational but not too demanding. Hence I could concentrate on my studies in the evenings. When the year was up, I was allocated to the Architect's Department. Administrative assistants must expect to experience a number of departments. So I was less than surprised to leave education.

It was a new set of tasks for me as well as a new department. The staff were an assortment of characters. As a trainee administrator I worked under an administrative officer, a lady in her fifties. She was a good sort and I came to like her. The rest of the staff were clerical officers, who seemed to me to illustrate a variety of frustrations. The work had to do with administrative aspects of building and I doubt if any of the clerical workers found it particularly interesting. Probably because of this, there was a good deal of chatter and it was this which revealed the frustrations. There was a young man of about five-foot-nothing whose interest in a youthful female officer was generally rejected. Another young man was a failed-BSc who felt he was treated inconsiderately in the office. Another female clerical officer would have been perhaps in her later thirties. Her boy-friend was keen to marry her but was waiting for a divorce. This was as much a problem to the young lady officer as it was for him. Not that we ever saw him, only the lady officer who was tired of waiting. There was too, another young man and a black immigrant, who seemed to be accepted by all concerned. Another lady officer who seemed willing to talk about her lack of a proper home, tended to keep herself to herself. Finally, there was a lady in her fifties who took a delight in being as rude as possible to the office manager. I imagine that she was very frustrated over something but never found out what. Nor should I forget myself in the list of frustrations. I made no secret of the fact that I did not like clerical work. My guess is therefore that I added to the frustrations of the office. Overall, I think I added to the less than happy situation.

My reason for listing the above dissatisfactions is that I wonder how applicable this is to other office situations. Certainly, office situations vary. I found happy offices in County Hall and others where work commitment was most prominent. Even so, it seems useful to remember that the office as a work place is not necessarily a place of satisfaction.

However, my own frustrations were coming to an end – at least I thought they were. Now 34, I had found out what I wanted to do – my vocation that is. I would seek a job in teaching. I was not particularly interested in children. Rather, my aspirations lay in further or higher education. It was the experience of studying for a degree that had created the vocational answer. I had found the study of sociology fascinating, and felt that I was still young enough to be eligible to find a job teaching at that level. I did not expect to find a university lectureship. But at that time, polytechnics, combining technical, administrative and degree studies, were also available. If I failed to find a vacancy at this level, there were still technical colleges offering a wide range of school, technical and administrative studies. My work dilemma seemed solved because I had found what work to aim for. Moreover, I knew why I had found the answer. I had had to change, to become to some extent a different person. Learning sociology had changed me!

So I was seeking a job in education and I was very happy to leave clerical work.

Chapter Ten

The Education Saga

I give education a chapter to itself because it has been central to my life. My first college job was 1964. I was appointed as a lecturer in general studies at Letchworth College of Technology. The college taught a wide range of subjects covering science, technology, catering and administration. The highest qualification it taught for was Higher National Diplomas. At the lower end were a range of crafts and skills and it was with lads and lasses from these courses that I had to cope. General studies was part of their courses, the aim being to broaden the outlook of the students and avoid courses narrowly relating to technical skills.

My introduction consisted of a session sitting-in to a class of general studies taken by the teacher-librarian. The session lasted an hour and was for me an eye-opener. He was obviously an experienced teacher but he found it difficult to maintain order. At one point he told one misbehaving lad to leave the classroom. I learned later that this is not an acceptable option for general studies teachers since many of the lads are day-release students (released from an employer) who will happily head off home if they get the chance. If this were discovered by the employer the college would soon be in trouble. Each day-release lad was expected to receive his day-long dose of education per week.

The perspective of the lads was likely to be very different. They were involved in technical courses of various kinds. To them, general studies was simply a wasted hour. There would be no general studies in the examination they would sit at the end of their course. So why should they bother with this subject? Education policy might want a technical training to be broadened into education. But the views of educational policy-makers was no matter of interest to the lads. Their view of education was largely instrumental. To them, education was a means to certification. They needed the qualification in order to keep their jobs and/or to make progress in employment. But general studies did not feature in this perspective.

Such attitudes made life difficult for the general studies teacher. He or she had further problems. There were female students as well as the lads. These teenage girls would be on catering courses for example. But though less rowdy, the girls were no more enamoured of general studies than the lads. However, there was one other very important group to consider – the staff. In this regard, one should bear in mind that the college was largely technological in its teaching. Hence, the staff were dominantly technological in their background and teaching. Their view of general studies was no different than the lads. To these staff, general studies was simply a waste of time and the staff who taught it lacked all credence. No wonder that general studies was little better than a joke in this college, and doubtless other colleges too. I suspect that technical colleges and Further Education in general is a cultural wasteland. Discussions with other staff in other colleges supports this view.

How then might general studies be taught at all? Each teacher of the subject had to learn about the lads and lasses. The background of the boys was usually some kind of interest in engines, particularly motorcycle engines. The girls seemed mostly to be considering finding jobs, e.g. in catering, hairdressing, reception or shop work. I saw no burning interest between the sexes. The lads mainly saw the girls as useful for sticking on the back of a motorbike because that augmented status in the male culture.

Given this situation, it seems worth repeating: how could one teach the subject? The general studies teachers found various answers. One approach would be to tack as much onto their interest in engines as possible. One could consider the manufacturers, the skills required for operation, the types of engines and so on. To these issues one could contrast manufacturers in North and South of Britain, their surrounding economic conditions. Or one could compare economic conditions for motorcycle manufacturers in different countries. A different approach would be to raise issues currently in the mass media: types of crime, contrasting issues of heterosexuality and homosexuality, or race issues related to immigration into Britain.

One could usually drum up interest in this way. The lads were generally of friendly disposition and were willing to be provoked into discussion – provided they realised that the teacher was keen to stir some interest. But, as indicated, general studies had to be oriented towards the lads' interests. If the teacher thought he or she could deliver a straight talk on the nature of politics or the nesting habits of birds, he or she would be in for a hard time – cat-calls, silly remarks, rival conversations among student groups and so on. Given the orientation of subjects towards their interests, the students were usually willing to engage in participative discussion.

Of course what I have said relates to the 1950s and 1960s. Matters may have since changed. I have no experience of general studies since that time. But one or two points can be made. The importance of the subject has increased. The world has become a good deal more interactive. World consciousness is developing or has already developed. Caring and other health skills have multiplied. Reports, memoranda, letters have increased as needed items of much shop floor work. The needs for a range of skills is today greater than my era of general studies teaching. Further Education should have responded to this. General studies should have developed in appropriate ways and increased in relevance to the lads and lasses whose approach might well be narrowly focused on their day-to-day task.

Let me refer back now to technical college student culture. Although it is necessary to understand such a culture I would agree with those educationists who seek to change it. There is a need for a much broader perspective on life. But how can day release students be enabled to accept learning which lacks application towards any early financial return? And the technical staff too -- how can they be helped to recognise the value of the social sciences, history and the arts generally? Humbly, I suggest opening up the cultural horizons of these young people through discussions, visits to local places of interest and invited speakers from outside activities. This is general studies as liberal studies, as it is sometimes referred to. But it should be an examined course so that students take it seriously. I believe that this would also affect the attitudes of the technical staff of the colleges, though some would resent the subject even more, especially if they thought that students could fail an entire course if they failed the liberal studies examination. But that issue could be assigned to each college to decide.

One or two points I should add at this stage. We moved to Stevenage New Town in 1962. My wife, had secured a job there as a secondary school teacher and this meant that we were able to acquire a house. All the while, I was maintaining my studies and qualified in 1964 with a 2:2 BSc(Soc).

After three years in my first college job I sought to transfer my teaching to the developing polytechnic world. It was the era of the binary system in higher education. The aim of this system was to set up polytechnics alongside the universities in order to broaden the academic focus of higher education curricula by introducing a range of more vocationally oriented studies which polytechnics would provide.

Now let me return to the issue of my studies. When I graduated with the BSc (Soc), I realised that I should need more than this to enter higher education. Further study required a qualifying examination. With that out of the way I could proceed with a two-year part-time MSc.(Econ) course, for which I graduated in 1968. I specialised in industrial sociology, drawing on my experience as a chef in catering.

As soon as I learned that I could add MSc(Econ) to my qualifications, I began applying for posts in polytechnics. I was appointed a lecturer in sociology at Birmingham Polytechnic in 1968 and soon became a senior lecturer. I had a number of courses to teach covering health visiting, social work, social science and business studies. There were also external degrees of London University and these the Polytechnic set about changing to ones approved by the Council for National Academic Awards soon known by its initials (CNAA). This was a body brought together to ensure that degree standards were maintained by the polytechnics. CNAA soon became a frequent visitor to the polytechnics to approve and/or reject courses offered as degrees. Visiting panels were largely drawn from the universities. Initially, the polytechnic courses offered were often turned down which meant that they required resubmission, and this could lead to acceptance or further resubmission. It was a wearing procedure but I found I could cope.

Meanwhile, my studies were continuing. I had now registered for a PhD in sociology, specialising again in industrial sociology with a study of chefs and cooks comparing those in hospital catering with those in the commercial sector. This involved interviewing the staff employed in cooking in both sectors. The degree was awarded in 1972. I moved to Sunderland Polytechnic the following year, now as a principal lecturer. This polytechnic was well developed in the sciences and now wanted to promote the social sciences and arts. So I was quickly involved.

The staff grew in number as did the courses. My specialism in industrial sociology did not prove specially relevant and I found myself moving over to the family and race/ethnicity. Developing sociology proved demanding and I, like others in my position, soon found that CNAA's suggestion that new courses could try new perspectives was somewhat dangerous, since these perspectives would be examined by professors with well-developed views about what sociological courses should look like. Basically, the approval system for sociological degrees and the like (e.g. economics, politics, business studies) was a power structure in which established professors said what sociology was, leaving little room for alternative approaches. The safest answer was to follow established approaches and this led to success for those who did and rejection for those who did not. Being in the latter category I soon found myself less than appreciated. Where courses failed to gain CNAA approval the Polytechnic's support for staff was apt to diminish. So began my loss of appreciation as a leading member of staff. This was accompanied by a similar loss of appreciation among colleagues. My ambition as a sociologist was stalled.

Let me brighten the situation with a timely tale. I had agreed to return a batch of projects for a colleague since I was about to teach the students concerned. I found the projects heavy and put them on the floor outside the lecture theatre door. I had expected to return them to the students once I was ready to deliver my lecture. However, as I arrived at the door, a batch of students came pouring out. Forced to wait, I edged the projects on the floor, away from the feet of the exiting students. To do so, I had to bend down. Unbeknown to me, as I did so my clip-on braces unsnapped. It was not long before my students were in the lecture theatre and I had returned the projects. I was soon into my subject – observation. I was making some vigorous arm movements to emphasise points when I began to realise that my trousers and I were parting company. This must have been the sole lecture I have ever given where my hands were throughout in my pockets. This was the only way I could prevent my giving some unexpected illustration to the subject of observation.

The polytechnic era came to an end in the 1990s when they became universities. The change of name was sensible because they had acquired degree-level courses in the sciences, technologies, arts, literature, etc. At the same time, the universities copied the polytechnics where they had succeeded, e.g. in business studies. Hence most polytechnic s simply took on the university title.

I had been in polytechnic education since 1973. The job consists of university lecturing, marking student work and research. The lectures really depend on careful reading and note-taking. It is important to make the subject interesting while delivering the facts. Marking tends to be tedious but requires care and thought. Research is fascinating but often requires money which is apt to be difficult to obtain. Without money one is forced to carry out one's own researching. That is very time-consuming. Because of this, small projects are apt to be preferred but even for these money is apt to be sought yet is far from easy to acquire. Large scale research is apt to be government sponsored and assigned to well-known named researchers and universities. Finally, there is administration, e.g. collating marks, attending boards of assessment and so on – tedious but necessary.

I retired in 1991 and set about establishing a University of the Third Age ('U3A' as we call it) in my town of retirement – Worthing. U3A is an organisation established all over the UK and many other countries for the purpose of providing low-cost teaching on many and varied subjects. The teachers of these subjects are persons of relevant knowledge while local participants supply attendance. U3A is now a very successful organisation the world over.

After a year offering sociology, I began to feel that something was missing. I sought greater involvement of my audience. Participants were too much attendees – persons who sat in on the lecture and discuss issues raised by the lecturer. But where was their experience and social learning called on? Curiously enough, I was at this time, using Sussex University library in order to keep up with references for my lectures. There I spied a notice about a one-year course entitled Life History Work. I was happy to sign up to it. As this was completed I added life story writing to the subjects I offered to U3A groups, at the same time starting a doctoral study on developing an autobiography. A DPhil. entitled *Autobiography and Life Review* was awarded in 1998. I continued to offer a life story writing group throughout the period 1994 – 2012. Some participants completed in a year but most people tended to take two or more years. The course became popular and I found myself offering two groups of around 8-10 participants in some years.

How would I assess the learning which participants derived? Firstly, I would regard the reflective process, which life story writing engenders, as an important exercise. When people think about their lives a process of self-assessment occurs. I regard this as a valuable exercise even if that assessment is biased in favour of the writer. Even where that bias is considerable, I would still support life story writing because it has induced self-evaluation. That has been a useful exercise on which the writer can later build – perhaps in the after-life.

Secondly, there is the discussion in the life-story writing groups. These groups become important learning bodies, sometimes helping a writer to re-evaluate his/her own story. The two findings above contribute importantly to what I came to call life review.

A further point worth making is to draw attention to the value of the life review groups. People often argue that they prefer to write on their own, frequently perhaps because they wish to hide aspects of their experience. However these efforts are apt to form a substantial part of abandoned autobiographies. A group helps to keep the activity going.

Basically, I enormously enjoyed my teaching career. The beginning was difficult because unexpected. The attitudes of day-release students to learning, (i.e. most learning outside their own technical matters), was off-putting. In practice it was a rejection of learning of any kind, other than the minimum required to fulfil that which was necessary for the employer. Such an attitude to learning came as a shock to me. However, looking back, I can see how valuable it was for me to understand such a perspective. The experience was an introduction to a culture utterly different to my own but which was nonetheless useful to grasp. Why? Because it was learning valued in terms of wages, an estimation unrecognised to those reared on university perspectives. Such an outlook will never be mine but I needed to recognise its existence.

The beginning was difficult because unexpected. I have acknowledged that attitudes of day-release students to learning, (i.e. most learning outside their own technical matters), was off-putting. However, looking back, I can see how valuable it was for me to understand such a perspective. To understand such a culture is not to accept it. It is the first step to a realisation of how much more important are those who espouse it than the narrow perspective they endorse.

My own family is considered next since it was an important influence in my life.

Chapter Eleven

Family

My wife wanted children but I could not have said that I was interested. When we first got married we could not have afforded them anyway. The position changed when my career was clearer, I had become a lecturer and we had secured a house in Stevenage, a new town in the South of England. I was able to find the mortgage since my salary was reasonable but in those days (the 1960s) one also had to have ten per cent of the price of the house in order to be accepted as a purchaser. Whenever we moved the same situation applied and it was always an embarrassment. We were eventually able to achieve the ten per cent in the end but it was never easy. Some people argue that the system was sensible since it prevents purchasers taking on a 100 per cent mortgage which they cannot really afford.

With the house secure, what about the baby? Because my wife had a medical history of TB as a teenager, we decided to try adoption. We applied to the local authority and were interviewed by a social worker. She was not happy with the fact that my work career revealed several changes. But it was my unwillingness to commit myself to the Church which finished the application. She argued that people need religion as a means of helping them through life. Since I was unwilling to consider any association with the Church, that was the end of that! Now to a point, a social worker must use her values. One would not expect him or her to accept a couple as reasonable for adoption who had failed in adoption elsewhere, though, as always, there might be exceptional circumstances. But to intrude values concerning religion would seem to me to be dangerous. Provided he or she is satisfied with a couple's home and family values, religious persuasion should not be a reason for acceptance or dismissal.

However, there seemed nothing we could do about it, so we accepted the need for procreation. All went well during pregnancy and then the time for birth arrived. Fortunately, my wife had elected for a hospital situation so the fact that it was a breach birth caused no particular difficulty. Our daughter appeared in October, 1966, though the first I knew about it was when I visited the hospital and a nurse handed me a white bundle wrapped in a shawl. I found it quite a shock. I was a father who had little considered his role. By this time, there was paid maternity leave so Barbara could have returned to teaching within a few weeks. However, in practice it was a few years before she did, during which time, the family depended, as do so many couples, on my income alone.

But money was not the biggest change. Lifestyle was bigger and the biggest aspect of this was the requirements of the child. When the two of you are on your own, you serve your partner and yourself. But when a third party appears, the entire lifestyle changes. It is not merely a matter of three to consider instead of two. It is the fact that that third person makes special demands and is accomplished at letting you know about its needs. These include feeding, preparing the milk for bottle-feeding, (in our case), cleaning the bottle, changing the nappy, and rocking the baby off to sleep. Add to this the way in which the family shopping changes due to the third party's needs and you have a reasonable picture of the changes imposed on the couple by the appearance of the additional person.

Alison would be our only child. We felt that we had started family building too late to add to the number. By the time our daughter had reached toddler stage, Barbara had found a job in a fee-paying school in Sunderland, while I lectured at the town's Polytechnic. Barbara's pupils were primary school age and this in fact seemed to suit Barbara well. It suited Alison well too. We had tried her in a nearby local school but she seemed very unhappy there. So the answer seemed obvious: let our daughter accompany her mother to her place of work – Sunderland Church High School. This was close to the section of the Polytechnic where I worked. So on weekdays, we all piled into the car together for the trip.

Alison soon warmed to this new school environment which seemed to suit her disposition. Private schools provided the kind of ambience to which she could settle, while developing her own innate capacities. Leadership qualities soon emerged and in due course, she became head girl. In this capacity she had, in her final year, to address a meeting of all the parents and children associated with the school in order to outline some of the school's activities. I simply could not have done this at her age but she took it all in her stride. Then on to university, which, so far as she was concerned had to be in London, where she settled down to read German at Kings College. This led to a year in Trier, a beautiful German town with a generally good climate. On return to Britain, there was a final year at halls of residence. She graduated with 2:1 honours. Within a year or two, she had met and married an Australian who was exploring living and working in England. Not long after the birth of a child, the couple left for long-term residence in Australia. Though her work is time-consuming, she kept in touch with my wife and I, her parents.

What I must now consider is my quality of fatherhood. It was not good. I was too wrapped up in my own work and my own studies. Moreover, with both my wife and our daughter attending the same school they could share experiences to which I had nothing to contribute. It is no surprise then that closeness was not part of my family life. However, perhaps I may add that, in my view, the first child is very much a learning experience. My quality of fatherhood might well have improved by the time later children arrived. But as indicated, there were no later children for us, and I should acknowledge that I did not seek more offspring.

We now experience the family only at a distance and this has been so since our daughter (with a granddaughter) accompanied her husband back to Australia. We have contact by telephone, however, and they visit us every few years. So we have been able to watch our granddaughter growing up and moving from school to university. Our daughter was able to gain employment in a human resources agency in Australia. She is chief executive in this agency, while her husband operated a building firm specialising in the upkeep of homes. I have to use the past tense for him since he died in 2013, a brain tumour and cancer victim.

How do I evaluate my family experience? I needed someone to love and that my wife provided. We were a loving couple. As our daughter grew up she took much of our attention. As indicated, mother and daughter attended the same school, albeit in different capacities. Not surprisingly, the school became the focus of attention in our home so that, increasingly, I became more of a domestic onlooker rather than a participant. My wife and I were still reasonably close when our daughter departed. At the time of writing (2014), my wife has died. She was suffering from alzheimer's disease and this is thought to have led to disinterest in food and drink. That disinterest proved fatal.

I am moving towards my final years but before I end my account I should consider a key figure in my life – the Count de Santi.

Chapter Twelve

A key influence

There has really only been one key person of influence in my life. His name when I met him was Leslie Bancroft. But as I said earlier, after his removal to France, he took over his father's title and became the Count de Santi. He played the key role mentioned earlier of providing somewhere for me to live so that I could leave home. However, he was really a far greater influence than this hospitality might suggest. He brought Theosophy into my life, the Masters and the Arcane School.

I met him at regular meetings of the Theosophical Society in London. Both my brother and I found him easy to talk to and able to discuss theosophical issues. On taking up residence in his flat in Pimlico, we came to know him as a charismatic figure. He had built up a group of people who would visit him from time to time, especially for the group meetings. At these meetings he would read sections from the Secret Doctrine. But after some months, this was replaced by readings from Alice Bailey's Treatise on Cosmic Fire. This activity was supplemented by lectures and provision of 'spirit messages' for various meetings of the Spiritualist movement.

This latter was not a group activity; merely an activity for the Count who acted as a medium and to which I would sometimes accompany him.

It seemed to me that it was the Masters who suggested that he move the group, (of which I was a member), in favour of the Arcane School and we all joined. He himself joined after meeting Alice Bailey who was on a visit to G.B. at the time. I am unsure what level he joined at but whatever it was, he had to produce written answers to questions, as did the rest of us. In due course, it became clear that the perspective in his answers was one of expecting acceptance of his point of view. However, the Bailey approach to the secretaries (who assess student work) was one which supported the Tibetan's writings. But the Count was none too willing to accept correction. The crunch came with the term *culture*. He would not accept the Tibetan's perspective of the term.

This built on earlier disagreements with the result that he was dismissed from the Arcane School. I think he found this a shock! In fact, his departure from the School over the conceptual dispute may have been just as well. He was a homosexual who believed homosexuality helped to foster a formless consciousness which heterosexuality did not since this was based on attraction between forms. But the Tibetan regards homosexuality as one of the "sexual excesses" left over from Lemuria. He classes it as a problem to be healed, though he does exempt hermaphroditism from this perspective (Esoteric Healing, Lucis Press, 1978, 62-64).

Yet the Tibetan makes various references to HPB (who compiled the Secret Doctrine) as 'he' thought her body was basically female. He also recognises polarity and the spiritual aspect of sexuality and ends *A Treatise on Cosmic Fire* by reference to "the marriage song of the Heavenly Man" (TCF, 1283). Further, it has long been the teaching in theosophical circles that karma affects the choice of male or female body. It follows that some Egos with a history of incarnation in male physical bodies who found themselves in a female one for karmic reasons, might consider adjustment to a homosexual outlook. However, the Tibetan's viewpoint might most likely be that the current extent of homosexuality has little or nothing to do with the provisos I have suggested.

The Count's special quality was his ability to work creatively with people. I often watched him in the process of conversation. He would enter into the world of the other person and during the stages of interaction, would draw out the best in them. This activity was most noticeable on the feeling level. One of his intriguing aspects was that he did not identify with form. This enabled him to disregard his own body. Indeed, he was able to forget himself during interaction with others. Thus his own personality was used as a foil to enable him better to understand the nature of the other person and his/her attitudes and values. In these situations, his own self became simply a tool. Moreover, he seemed able to share the feelings of others. Their failed romance was his; their experience of poverty and insecurity was his, their loss of esteem was his too. Thus he was able to identify with the experiences of those with whom he worked by using his own difficult background as a means of sharing the other persons' experience.

He had a down-to-earth pragmatic mind which was enlightened by an intuitional insight into matters. The concept of the intuition is often considered controversial. I would explain it as a kind of mind which can approach issues by expressing thought which has not been subject to a period of ratiocination. Intuition depends on an expression of deep understanding rather than a period of mental activity. The Count was not an intellectual. His formal education ended with his school days.

He dressed badly, though this mattered little since his background of an upper middle class home afforded him that easy-going charm which almost instantly crosses barriers. In a group situation he would use his outstanding quality of personalised impersonal attention on any he chose to work with. Equally, he would simply ignore any brash attention-seeker out to claim special attention. As a platform speaker, he had a style which put him quickly in touch with those present.

As a young man, he had had TB. He would mention this occasionally but it seemed to be unimportant in middle age. For example, we knew him as a keen tennis player. He was also a keen bridge player. In fact, many of his days would be passed in play with imaginary bridge competitors. In the evenings, the groups would gather and discussion would usually take over. These were apt to become heated in which he would often take up a particular position where others would give prominence to quite different perspectives.

It is important too, to mention his association with the Masters. They would often use him as a medium. One or other of them would take over his consciousness, while he became a mere listener, like the rest of the group. A Master would then use his (the Count's) mental apparatus to deliver a message or engage in conversation with the group. Such conversations were mostly brief. The messages could be longer but usually not by very much. The form of these interventions was similar to those of the Tibetan in Alice Bailey's Discipleship in the New Age, Vol. I, 1944 and Vol. II, 1955 and later editions, (London, Lucis Press).

Some readers will wonder how we, the listeners, knew who the Masters were. How did the group know that he was the Master he declared himself to be? Surely this is relevant when one recalls that the Count was a former actor. But his thought and spoken form of words was of a simpler, less profound quality than that of a Master. Moreover, there were occasional occurrences which were revealing. For example, one of the group once sat in the Count's chair when the latter was not present. Instantly, this group member was taken over by what the Spiritualists call 'spirits' and began delivering what I took to be 'spirit messages'. He was soon prized out of the chair by another group member and he quickly 'came round', knowing nothing of his experience.

The Count's removal to France ended most of my association with him. However, after a couple of years in Paris, he asked me to join him. I was reluctant but he became insistent. The trip proved valuable because it revealed another aspect of his character. His dwelling was a flat in a large block. The whole place struck me as a down-at-heel flea pit. Had he been able to remove the bed bugs and fleas I doubt the place would have remained standing. None of this seemed to worry him. He found the other inhabitants interesting people and took the view that if he rented a more up-market place, the current inhabitants would not be present. In fact, he may not have been able to afford anything better. Even so, it was certainly the case that he would talk about the other residents and show interest in their backgrounds and current situation. He had accommodated to the lifestyle of the poor and was content with it. This seems to me entirely praiseworthy. The people mattered; their conditions did not. However, I should acknowledge that his situation was not to my taste. Nor was his homosexuality; I returned home the following day.

It is time to sum up on the Count. So far as I was concerned he was a very valuable source of light by helping me to understand my home situation. Sometimes people have said to me that a trained counsellor could have done the job as well. But a trained counsellor would have wanted payment – money which I did not have. His homosexuality does not fit the good life which we, as would-be disciples are urged to follow. But as the Tibetan says, the Masters must accept the forms of lifestyle they are offered however misconceived, provided what they are offered is of an adequate standard of consciousness. So I would accept the view that the Count was what he said he was -- a fourth degree initiate. He is no longer with us; he died in his seventies in Paris some time in the 1970s.

I have discussed the individual who had special meaning for me. But there were also subjects which were equally important and these need consideration too. These matters are next to be considered.

Chapter Thirteen

Motivating Influences

I felt it necessary to consider dominant motivating factors in my life. There have been four. One has already been touched on as the life story developed: the key religious-philosophical theme starting with Theosophy, moving the Arcane School and concluding with the Morya Federation. The actual content of concern has been the writings of Alice Bailey which features the work of the Tibetan. The internet is the quickest source to provide more material on these three. However, there are three other motivating factors: music, sociology and the University of the Third Age. I plan to deal with these in turn.

It was the Count who introduced me to music by tuning into radio broadcasts during my various visits and eventual stay with him. To me it was a new world. My first experience was the work of Wagner and this was followed by the popular classical writing of predominantly Nineteenth Century composition: Mozart, Beethoven, Brahms and other well known composers of that era. I found all this utterly absorbing and had little time for the Twentieth Century. However, this situation gradually changed as I came to appreciate Sibelius, much of whose work belongs to the earlier years of that century. Also Mahler, whose work like Sibelius overlaps into this later century. I was busy adding more names to the early Twentieth Century when I realised that I was really dealing with an era, a particular period of outstanding musical composition covering the two centuries. At the moment, I can see little to suggest that this extends into the Twenty-first Century. I do not believe that electronic music (e.g. Boulez) is such an extension. Nor Schonberg with his twelve tone scale. But we shall see.

The composers of the later Twentieth Century and the Twenty-first do not seem to me to be outstanding. Benjamin Britten in England, Philip Glass in the USA, Olivier Messiaen in France are not for me the equal of Igor Stravinsky, let alone the names earlier listed in the Nineteenth Century. I believe that I am not alone in suggesting that we await a new era of great musical composition.

Let me move on to consider the relevance of sociology, which we might define as the study of social influences on human behaviour. I chose sociology for my masters degree -- even though it is labelled MSc(Econ), because economics is the dominant discipline. Stephen Cotgrove led the subject at London's Regent Street Polytechnic and certainly provoked my interest, as he did that of many others. The discipline enabled me to complete two doctoral degrees - a PhD and a DPhil. The DPhil is entitled *Autobiography and Life Review*, (University of Sussex, 1998). In the final chapter I seek to consider the ideas behind life review. This latter term seeks to look at the assessment of one's life and is therefore central to the project of learning. The value of this is that it might usefully be applied to the life story as it is being written or subsequently.

There are a number of stages. At the start, there needs to be an orientation of reflectiveness and this reflectiveness needs to embrace a readiness for imagination. Such an orientation is desirable in order to avoid some of the traps into which a superficial stance can carry the life reviewer. Permit situations under assessment to develop in their fullness. Issues and persons which may seem little relevant are best found a place in the overall assessment because they may turn out to be more important than they at first appear. Imagination is valuable because there will often be more than one assessment to consider: your own, those of others present on the occasion or over the continuing situation. These varying assessments will themselves need to be boiled down into one or more evaluations, which can be held more or less tentatively. Hence the need for imagination.

Someone contemplating the writing activity might at this stage wonder where the energy will come from and even if it emerges, whether it will stay the course? From my own experience of the autobiography group I have found that a sense of commitment can be generated from recollections of a dilemma. Further dilemmas can help to move the work on and this helps to generate persistence. However, there is no doubt in my mind that the most important single factor enabling continuing persistence is the presence of a group. Members feel a sense of obligation to others in the group and wish to avoid "letting the group down". The second most important factor of stimulation is the group leader.

Some people might wonder if therapy would help – saving a failing chapter because it has just reached a stage where the writer wishes to duck a phase he preferred to forget. This might be so, but it is useful to recall that life story writing is itself a therapy because it enables the writer to face up to himself in the context of a sympathetic group. It is crucial for the group leader to see that his groups are exactly that – sympathetic. At the very least members must offer understanding.

One might ask now where does the reflectiveness, imagination, persistence, etc. lead us, lead the writer?

Hopefully, to the goal of creativity! What are the influences on that? The answer would seem to be – just about everything. But certainly, the circumstances are important. For example, there must be some money available, or else the first step must be to achieve some. Secondly, the person makes a substantial difference.

However, what matters most is: how can creativity be stimulated? One might consider the first step to be systematic thought and reasoning. Moreover, reflectiveness and imagination are now able to focus on an issue or a situation – all the items of context. And an important element of the context is the group. If individuals can become creative, so can groups. The result can be twofold: meaning eventuates and the person or persons involved experience development. In other words, the person grows mentally and quite possibly grows spiritually as well and the soul enters his thought and action.

What I have sought to show above is that sociology (and doubtless many other disciplines) can be of practical use to the life story writer. It provides him with a means of developing his ideas concerning what to write, and it develops him as a person.

Now let me take up the last of the four motivating factors as I have called them – U3A. Earlier I indicted that this became important when I retired. It became important in the DPhil as I drew on recordings of some the life story writing groups to illustrate the above arguments. However, let me here take up some of the broader sociological aspects drawn from group studies of current issues. Examples would often be drawn from current issues, especially as these featured in the mass media: dementia, the changing nature of crime, leading female figures in politics, the pros and cons of the European Union, the future of the National Health Service, and so on. These issues usually provoked a good discussion. I would supply several pages of written material which I read out in order to start the meeting, which was then thrown open for members to take up aspects relevant to them or related to their reading on the matter. These were involving for members and for me. As a weekly experience it was enjoyable and, I believe, informative.

Another sociological approach was based more directly on the nature of the discipline. This took the form of seeking to show how social situations influenced people. Earlier the point was made that there is a general lack of recognition of just how far we are all influenced by the circumstances of our lives. People will agree in general this must be so. But seek to use social influences to explain some aspect of character or behaviour and it soon becomes apparent that what is most prominent in someone's mind is their own personal outlook and orientation. There may be difficulty in recognising that this personal outlook is itself the product of social influences. Certainly people vary in their nature from birth but social experience massively influences how their behaviour develops.

Lastly, let me turn to the University of the Third Age, which its members know by the initials U3A. Where did the idea come from? Initially from France were it was established in 1973, emerging from the early 1980s in Britain. The history of the movement is described in various places e.g. Francis Beckett, *The U3A Story*, 2014. Its groups can be found in countries the world over.

I was able to develop both my sociology and my life story writing through it, twenty happy years. Older people join it once they hear of it. One might say that it should advertise more but advertising costs money and the organisation, both at local and national level, seek to keep the costs down. My guess is that it mainly attracts by word of mouth and this seems mostly to enable it to flourish. Thus in my town of 100,000 people, U3A has over 500 members. Both sexes are well represented though women are inclined to predominate. Subjects are put forward by anybody who feels that they have a topic or specialism to offer. These mostly extend over a year or more, based on a weekly, fortnightly or monthly gathering and operate in local rooms or in members' own accommodation. The annual charge varies according to the U3A, the sums differing from a few pounds to perhaps £20 or more depending at least partly on the extent and quality of material produced.

The latter varies considerably. So does the number of subjects offered. Twenty or thirty is common enough but more is possible and so is less. A few examples are: history (limited in operation to a particular period or situation), literature, (again limited in practice to a particular topic or writer), films, photography, various languages, story telling, play reading, philosophy, etc.; card games, such as bridge are likely to be on offer too. Thirty of more subject groups are common enough. U3A members use it variously. Some will be members of a group every day of the week. For others, group participation is once or twice a week, while still others are no more than occasional attenders over the year.

So we have completed the four dominating issues of my life. Hence it is time now to review the life as a whole and reconsider the nature of the exercise.

Chapter Fourteen

Last thoughts

My final chapter aims to be an assessment of key points of learning in my life. This is crucial because, as earlier indicated, I take the view that we come back many times in order to learn. To learn what? To be the soul rather than personalities who are made up of affection and selfishness, pleasure seeking and kindness, some powers of thought but limited wish to use it, concern for our physical form often unsupported by attention to lifestyle, and so on. Personalities vary in how they present themselves to the world but most of them are basically concerned with the satisfaction of the individual person. However, everyone also has a soul and aspects of it appear from time-to-time in our lives. I take the view that we need to enhance the place of the soul in our lives. By so doing we would make the world a far happier place in which to live for billions of people. Wars would cease and everyone, everywhere, would have the opportunity to grow into fulfilled individuals, groups and societies.

How do we enhance the presence of the soul in our lives? By deepening our concern for others and by seeing that this becomes a central focus in our lives. Over many lives we learn to do this. The sooner we live unselfishly the more we move towards world improvement. That is the goal for people everywhere. When that is achieved a new goal of spiritual living will take over. But that, for most of us is a distant goal. Yet we must learn to move towards it as a present goal because we otherwise set it aside as "something for tomorrow", "a too distant goal", "something for my next life". The lure of procrastination is endless.

We may sometimes wonder how the personality was formed in the first place. The answer lies in social learning. As our faculties grew and our bodies enjoyed growth so we were exposed to the attitudes and values of those around us. This is often accompanied by a tendency to underrate the nature and extent of what is termed socialisation. Initially, the family is the dominant influence. But before long school provides an additional influence together with other children in our neighbourhood, some of whom become friends. As teenagers we often acquire additional relationships and will have undergone a fair amount of structured learning to which many young people will add more social learning from the university sector. Thus there is formal and informal learning from our environment from the word 'go'.

Yet we are all different. Children brought up in the same family are distinct, even if they have some traits in common. If you recognise reincarnation, these differences are not difficult to explain. We each have hundreds of different former lives. Hence our differences in this life.

How can we distinguish the personality? To build on the point just made – personalities differ. Many are generally pleasant to meet. Others are less so while some are gruff and perhaps even malevolent. But all or nearly all, are characterised by the general quality of selfishness. This is over and above the need to take care of the self. Selfishness is characterised by the overall wish to enhance the self in its many aspects of existence. There will often be an accompanying degree of unselfishness. Yet selfishness is the overall guiding quality of the life.

Contrast this with the soul and its overall quality of unselfishness – which arises from its perception of the One Life. What is the idea behind this term? Life has many forms which change over time. Yet each form is conscious in some way. The view is that all forms share life and that this potency of life is ultimately one, even though it takes different forms within the kingdoms. Moreover, it is said to be possible to realise this one life. This is possible when we achieve soul consciousness. The soul understands how despite the many differences within and between the kingdoms and between people the sense of life is shared and can be known or can be registered because the soul is not cut off from other kingdoms while personalities and physical bodies are.

Humankind is evolving towards soul consciousness. But personality is still dominant in most people's consciousness yet there is some measure of soul outlook. Reincarnation is one of the principal means whereby evolution takes place. Eventually, the soul will take over and most people will grow used to down-playing their personality awareness. However, for the present and for some time to come, personalities are likely to dominate and we shall need to appeal to that which we believe is best in people so that we can achieve the highest forms of awareness.

In fact we are all capable of seeking soul consciousness in ourselves and in others. There will be times when we shall find it and times when we do not but I suggest that we should always seek it. Of course, many of our interactions with others scarcely permit of an approach seeking a soul response. But if our goal is soul consciousness, that will find opportunities when deeper discussion becomes possible. It is this insight that led me to return to the Arcane School once I had retired.

There will be some people who seek to move forward now. They have no wish to wait or maybe they have grown tired of delay and are awaiting a chance to enter more concentrated study. There are many places in the world offering local groups supported by persons with strong commitment to a more spiritual way of life. Where these seem not yet to exist there are the movements earlier named: The Theosophical Society, The Arcane School, The Morya Federation. These can be sought via the internet. Browsing there will supply various other sources.

In this last chapter there is another crucial subject I must tackle: how should one approach autobiographical writing? I am not seeking a discussion of the particular needs of writing about a life. That exists and again, I would refer anyone interested to the internet. My concern is with issues that make life story writing worth doing. The first issue in this connection might be called telling the truth. Again I would wish to avoid philosophical debates about what the truth is. What I mean might be best described by the phrase 'telling it like it was'. One can either write the section, dealing with a particular event, as closely as one can recall it, and then evaluate it. Or one can seek to evaluate it without a lengthy description of the happening. But if you prefer the latter method you would be wise to seek to recall all the detail of motivations, often conflicting, of yourself and any others who might have been involved. It is important to recognise that often you will be involved in situations where the conflict of motivations is your own as well as that of others. What is so important is the need to recognise the complexity of issues and how you finally responded to them. Perhaps the painful issues will be the most difficult to cope with. Yet we must learn to cope with them because that is why we are here, as it were – to learn!

In relation to the above I will now seek to illustrate a problem I had to tackle when entering teaching. It will be recalled that my earliest venture was into a technical college where I was among the general studies teachers. Neither the students, nor the staff bore this subject any love. The students generally put up with it, while the staff sneered at it and those who taught it. Such a situation led me to the view that my commitment to ideas about reincarnation, the soul, etc. would be best quietly set aside. Yet could not these ideas have been introduced via issues of comparative religion? But would comparative religion have been a subject that the lads would have accepted for discussion when their interest was in motorcycles and their engines? Yet might not an able and experienced teacher have found approaches? Perhaps, but I was not at that stage an experienced teacher.

Yet even if this is considered an adequate answer were there no ways of introducing the philosophical issues when I was established in the Polytechnic? Buddhism was being offered as an interest by one of the lecturers. Could not I have offered my Arcane School studies? Unfortunately, because I had dropped these studies in my youth I should have needed to have spent a lot of time catching up. However, this could have been done, instead of joining the Buddhist group – which I did – in order to share some aspects of my commitment to Eastern thought. I will leave the matter there because I have sought to use this issue to illustrate the complexity of motives. Some people will say that I took an easy way out. Others will argue that I opted for sensible policies. What matters is that I should be able to reach a conclusion and avoid glossing over the entire issue.

Another issue raised by the various chapters' discussions might be said to be how far should I have concerned myself with the quality of the writing? My answer is that unless you are an established author, all that matters about the quality of the writing is that it is understandable. Most autobiographies are not published. Hence failure to publish need not be an issue. Indeed, in most cases there is no point even in trying to publish. Why then did you write it? To help you to understand your life. That is the point. If you put it on the internet, others can read it too. That might lead to discussion and possibly greater understanding. But pick your listener with care. Yet should you not be indifferent to the opinions of others? In some respects – yes, since it is useful to remember that a thoughtful listener can offer help through questioning and discussion. But there will be others who seek merely to scoff and deride, perhaps to bolster their own sense of insecurity.

What should one's stance be during one's writing? To repeat: the best approach is to seek to avoid both condemning or condoning. Record events, thoughts and feelings, those of yourself and those of others so far as you were aware of them. Explain if your views have changed over time, and of course, explain why. But it is important not to become embroiled in what happened because if they were personality experiences you will recreate some situation all over again to no useful purpose.

Issues of meaning are a further consideration. Maybe what was meaningful to you does not appear meaningful to others. When you discuss some event with others who were with you at the time, these others see no special importance in what happened. That does not matter. People's values and judgments vary. If you thought it important, give it all the attention you feel it deserves. One reason why others may not see some happening as significant, is because it generates a sense of failure, guilt or fear and these some persons wish to avoid. If you sense this, it is important to give it special attention while playing down the associated negative emotions.

A kind of opposite problem is that of memory. How far are you able to remember and remember accurately? I have found that one of the best means for stimulating memory is to write a synopsis of events. Arranging these in historical order is the next step. You may find this quite a challenge but bear in mind that once the synopsis of the autobiography is prepared, you can always go back to it and add events earlier forgotten. It follows from this argument that the first synopsis should be prepared before you begin the autobiographical writing.

The next question might be where do you start the story? One answer might be – with your earliest memories and then move progressively forward through childhood. In practice, my experience of life story writing over the years is that most people do exactly that.

But where **should** you start? The answer is wherever you prefer. Of course that means you will have to adjust the history as you develop the story. If you are a writer of some skill and some practice, adjusting your history is perhaps not really a problem. But most people are not writers, not accomplished ones anyway, so they prefer to follow the historical approach.

Who features in what you write? This is well worth considering because so many people seem to think that the very mention of somebody else, other than themselves, is dubious, even wrong. It is important to realise that this is simply a mistaken view. It arises from the fact that many people are largely unaware of the extent to which they are influenced by others. We are all the products of the massive influences of family, school, workplace, community groups and so on. It follows that not to write about other people in an autobiography would be a complete mistake. It is that others, probably many others, will feature throughout your writing and are absolutely essential to everything you write. If they feature importantly, see to it that you describe what you believe to be their perspective on events. You may even need to provide a character sketch of the person involved.

One issue remains and it is important. Some people will say I have no wish to give up my personality. I enjoy giving it all the time it needs. I will exercise the soul too when I feel the need. So be it. But there are many others who have grown tired of their personality and sense its superficiality. They seek something deeper, something which puts them more in touch with others, more in touch with the events which are shaping the world. I hope that my writing will prove of some use to them and help them better to understand how they might proceed.

Time now to evaluate my life, while explaining why I take the views that I do. My position is that I believe that our assessments should be based on the greater good of humanity. I should therefore seek to help others where I can and seek generally to align my outlook and activities to the service of others. Certainly, my service should be guided by a sense of brotherhood and what I do should seek to foster the same sense in them. I realise that many people will cherish personal goals of fulfilment (those of ambition, desire for wealth, or acclaim at work, even public acknowledgement) distinct from the above. Such are the goals of personalities. While acknowledging them I do not believe that they will benefit humanity. So I hope that personality goals will be accompanied by more service oriented ones.

Since I have given priority to my three dilemmas it would make sense to begin with consideration of my performance in that connection. The first was the sense that I needed to leave home, which both my brother and I did. My view is that we were right to do so. It led to a situation in which my mother re-evaluated her marriage, while her two sons had to accept the need to care for themselves – a need which both accepted.

A second dilemma was how I was to cope with conscription. Fortunately for me, I had found the arguments for refusing the call-up, the popular term for conscription. They were embodied in my new environment of the Count's flat. However, although I was convinced of my case at the age of eighteen, I am today less than certain. A successful fascist ideology would have been enormously difficult to remove had it taken over our society. The killing and maiming process of the war was horrible but the souls are not harmed and will return for further lives in due course. Moreover, new threats continue to emerge. I now consider that it is up to each person to consider whether he or she should take part in armed resistance to these threats. There is no general overall right policy towards the armed forces or political issues that apply to all situations. Individuals must assess each circumstance for themselves.

There remains dilemma number three – my pressing wish for interesting work. The venture into a career in cooking was not an adequate answer. The mind was presented with some relevant functions but only in a limited way. There was nothing to enable me to think about world circumstances. Yet I needed to be able to take part creatively in debates about world events. The first step was to improve my education. Maybe that would eventually also lead to more interesting work. My part-time study of higher education began in 1960 and completed in 1998 with the second doctoral degree. I realised I had found the answer in respect of interesting work. The light dawned half-way through the first degree in sociology: I should find work in teaching this fascinating subject.

Thus I had finally solved the three big issues of my life. But what of the others? Marriage and the family for example. Over the years, it was noticeable that my commitment to study lessened my interaction with my wife. Yet she had topics of interest: history, architecture and the theatre. These she retained but not to the point of deepening them. This I believe was her mistake. But it was mine too! Had I given her interests attention I could have helped to stimulate her intellectual potential throughout her life. That could have staved off the Alzheimer's from which she suffered in her eighties. The difficulty was that my own programme of studies made it difficult to find time for hers too. While that was true, there would have been time to chat about her interests had I seen the importance of so doing. I did find time for some attention to the family, but I think it would have benefited from rather more.

Another issue I should consider was my leaving my job on Peace News, the pacifist newspaper and the various commitments to non-violent demonstrations which were related to being at the heart of activity against nuclear weapons. I left to find a job which provided a better standard of living, having recently married, and for the same reason, I limited my involvement in demonstrations to avoid the dangers of a long prison sentence. I believe that I should have maintained my stance in relation to nuclear weapons, instead of disserting my friends who were demonstrating and going to prison for so doing. Some of the leaders of the anti-nuclear weapons at that time were absolutely outstanding people. There was Hugh Brock, the editor of Peace News, Harry Mister, Chris Farley, April Carter and a number of others. They cared about society and were prepared to experience prison to highlight the case against nuclear weapons. They were people of superb moral courage. I chose a different way, one which made little call on courage. I cannot return to the past but look forward now to a later chance to exercise their strength of character.

The last major event in my life was retirement in 1991. I was sixty-one. At the time of writing I am eighty-four. In those twenty-three years I have continued teaching, providing sociology seminars for U3A and life story writing groups. During this time, I spent over twenty years stimulating my U3A friends to write their autobiographies. This activity ended in 2013 when lack of physical strength no longer enabled me to offer home facilities as a meeting place. Nonetheless, I feel that this was a period of service to local people and would add this to the value of my polytechnic teaching career. My task since has been concerned with this autobiography, while continuing to teach and learn in the Morya Federation.

My hope is that I have stimulated others to write, or otherwise develop, their own life story.

Lightning Source UK Ltd.
Milton Keynes UK
UKOW04f2259310315

248891UK00002B/89/P